THE LIVING GOD

R. T. FRANCE

The Living God

INTER-VARSITY PRESS

INTER-VARSITY PRESS

Inter-Varsity Fellowship,
39 Bedford Square, London WC1B 3EY

Inter-Varsity Christian Fellowship,
Box F, Downers Grove, Illinois 60515

© INTER-VARSITY PRESS, LONDON
First edition October 1970

UK ISBN 0 85110 350 2
USA ISBN 0 87784 697 9

Printed in Great Britain by Hunt Barnard Printing Ltd, Aylesbury, Bucks.

CONTENTS

INTRODUCTION

This is a book of biblical theology. That may sound uninviting, even to Christians, who ought to know better. But theology is, according to the *Oxford English Dictionary*, 'the study or science which treats of God . . .'; and biblical theology is the study of what the Bible says about God. This is hardly a subject to which the Christian can be indifferent. Nor is it dull, as we shall see.

We shall not be studying what scholars have said about God, nor even what the church has taught. We want the Bible to speak for itself.

Nor shall we aim to be exhaustive. We trust there is no need to repeat well-known and well-loved truths, and still less the empty platitudes which often pass for theology. The wisdom of the publishers combines with the inclination of the author to limit our field of study to certain key ideas in biblical thought, ideas which we believe are as important as they are neglected in a lot of modern Christian thinking.

We are not concerned here with 'problems', at least not in the first instance. Not that there are no problems connected with the biblical teaching about God. But Christians are prone to spend too much time in looking at 'problems', and too little in getting to grips with the broad sweep of biblical thinking about God. Yet it is only by opening our minds to this breath-taking panorama of majesty that we are ever going to get into a position where we can see the problems in their true perspective. The lesson of Job still needs to be learned.

So this is not an academic treatise, nor even a textbook, on the doctrine of God. Such books are needed, and urgently needed now more than ever, but this is not one of them. This is a book of biblical theology, and whatever the Bible may be, it is certainly not academic. Indeed, this book is written with the conviction that the biblical teaching is above all experimental, practical, challenging, and exciting, and nowhere more so than in its portrayal of the central character, God.

Contemporary Christianity needs more theology! Not just the theology of the study and the library, but that truly *biblical* theology which makes God *real*, in experience as well as in theory. This was the theology of Moses and Isaiah, of Paul and John. Can anything less claim the title of 'biblical theology'?

1 THE LIVING GOD

It takes a lot to get theology into the headlines. As the powers that control the mass media are obviously aware, religion is not news. Perhaps the occasional religious riots, or a scandal involving a minister of religion. But certainly not theology.

But a few years ago even theology made a brief appearance on the front pages. The papers had only just got over announcing, 'Bishop's book that will shock thousands', when they carried the even more fascinating story of theologians who were apparently making themselves redundant by saying that God is dead.

And it is true: they are saying it, and meaning it. Christian theologians! And this in America, where a recent survey found that 97% believe in God, and 75% worship in church or synagogue at least once a month. Yet there in America, God is dead.

It is not our purpose here to expound or to evaluate the doctrine of the death of God – if indeed it can yet be tied down sufficiently to allow a systematic exposition: it is a phrase which has almost as many meanings as it has exponents. But its importance for us lies in the situation which has given rise to it. For it is perfectly true that for the vast majority of the church-going American population (and America is not alone in this distinction), God *is* dead.

It is not the whole story about the 'death-of-God' theologians, but it is at least one important aspect of their writing, that they are describing the true character of much contemporary Christianity. As far as the ordinary man in the pew is concerned, God is dead. His daily life runs its predictable, gilt-edged, humdrum course without reference to God. He would, of course, be scandalized by the suggestion that God is dead, but if it were true it would make no practical difference to his life. His work, his home, his sport, his politics, yes, and even his church life, would run on very much the same. They have no place for God; not practically, at any rate. God is a useful philosophical postulate, a comforting abstraction, a vague, nebulous word for what is solemn and serious and irrelevant to daily life. But He does not come into the reckoning when decisions are made, and the thought that He could have any practical effect on the way things turn out never disturbs the even flow of secular life.

C. S. Lewis found God to be 'the Transcendental Interferer'. The phrase would be meaningless to the vast majority of those who blithely recite, 'I believe in God, the Father Almighty . . .'. They might even find it irreverent. God is transcendent, certainly; but they would be hard put to it to think of the last time He interfered. They would not expect it. They would certainly not request it.

This, it seems, is at least a part of what the 'death-of-God' theologians want to say. They find it hard to see any practical difference between the life of the secularist and that of the Christian. They can find no suitable niche for God, as a practical proposition, in the life and thinking of modern man, whether he sports the cross or the sickle. And so they conclude that God is dead.

Their assessment, as we shall see, is profoundly biblical!

A God to be reckoned with

It will be the aim of this chapter to show that the God of the Bible is pre-eminently a God to be reckoned with. He is active, dynamic, irresistible. And His dynamic activity is not confined to the cosmic dimensions of a vast universe – that would be a relatively comfortable thought. But God is not comfortable. He is active no less in day-to-day human affairs, the petty concerns of microscopic man. He is relentlessly, uncomfortably present in the sordid business of commerce and war, of loving, living, and dying. He is 'the Transcendental Interferer'.

Or, to put it in the Bible's own words, He is *the living God*.

And when the Bible speaks of 'living', it is seldom, if ever, concerned with mere existence (as we shall see further below). 'The living God' is not a synonym for 'He who is', a metaphysical concept of God 'being there' (whether 'up there', 'out there' or anywhere else!). Life, in the Bible, means something vibrant and dynamic. It involves action. To speak of God as the living God is to make the daring claim that God is actively present here and now, a force to be reckoned with. If He is not that, then whether or not He exists is an academic question with which the Bible is not concerned; at least He would not be *living*, and that is what matters. If He were not living, He could not be God, in any sense that would mean anything to the men of the Bible. They would join with vigour in the ritual elegy, 'God is dead'.

But they say nothing of the sort. Their history and their experience, no less than their faith, compel them to proclaim the living God.

For the Hebrew this was one of the basic certainties of life. So certain was it, that he used it as a pledge for the truth of his word: 'as the Lord lives' (forty-three times). And lest it should be thought that this was a merely formal oath, used with no thought of its literal meaning, God Himself also confirms His word in the phrase, ' "As I live", says the Lord . . .' (twenty-three times). The veracity not only of the words of men, but of the very words of God, is staked on His being the living God. It is as basic as that.

The living God in the Old Testament

With such a build-up, it may come as a surprise to learn that the term 'the living God' is used only fifteen times each in the Old and New Testaments.[1] This is a warning to us against the old idea that a concordance alone is a sufficient tool for the study of a theme in biblical thought. When we have studied all the uses of a given word or phrase, we may have touched only the fringes of the *idea* which it embodies, which emerges in other words, in the narrative no less than in the explicit theologizing, throughout the whole fabric of biblical thought and history. So it is with the idea of the living God.

But the phrase itself may serve to lead us into the subject, and in fact its uses when taken together give a good insight into this dynamic idea.

Come then, first, to the bank of a river in spate. To the refugee rabble under the command of Joshua it forms an impassable barrier. But not to a man who knows his God. 'And Joshua said, "Hereby you shall know that *the living God* is among you . . . the waters of the Jordan shall be stopped from flowing, and the waters coming down from above shall stand in one heap" ' (Jos. 3:10ff.). And it happened, just like that. That is the sort of thing that happens when the living God is among you. You know about it. God is a force to be reckoned with.

[1] This includes the phrase 'the living Father' in Jn. 6:57.

Come now to a royal palace at daybreak. The king hurries with more urgency than dignity across the palace garden to the royal zoo, and cries out 'in a tone of anguish', 'O Daniel, servant of the living God . . .' – at least, that was what you claimed; but do the facts confirm it? Is He really the living God? '. . . Has your God, whom you serve continually, been able to deliver you from the lions?' He did not expect an answer, but it came, and with it the proof of Daniel's claim. And so the heralds went out to the distant provinces: 'I make a decree, that in all my royal dominion men tremble and fear before the God of Daniel, for he *is* the living God . . . he who has saved Daniel from the power of the lions' (Dn. 6:19-27).

Such a God is not one to be treated lightly, and certainly not one to be challenged to a duel. Yet that was just what two foolhardy men did. The first was Goliath. Poor man; he thought he was challenging one of the weakest armies in the league. But David knew better: 'Who is this uncircumcised Philistine, that he should defy the armies of *the living God*? . . . Your servant has killed both lions and bears; and this uncircumcised Philistine shall be one of them, seeing he has defied the armies of *the living God*' (1 Sa. 17:26, 36). Young David may not have looked much like 'the armies of the living God', but the proof of the pudding is in the eating.

Goliath perhaps did not know whom he was challenging. Sennacherib did. 'Then the Rabshakeh stood and called out in a loud voice . . .: "Thus says the king: '. . . Do not let Hezekiah make you to rely on the Lord by saying, The Lord will surely deliver us. . . . Who among all the gods of the countries have delivered their countries out of my hand, that the Lord should deliver Jerusalem out of my hand?' " ' (2 Ki. 18:28-35). Hezekiah was scared, as he had every political and military reason to be. But Isaiah would know the answer: 'It may be that the Lord your God heard all the words of the Rabshakeh, whom his master the king of Assyria has sent to mock *the living God*' (2 Ki. 19:4). Isaiah did know the answer, and Hezekiah was reassured. Then Sennacherib wrote a letter in the same vein, and this time Hezekiah took it straight to the Lord: 'Incline thy ear, O Lord, and hear; open thy eyes, O Lord, and see; and hear the words of Sennacherib, which he has sent to mock *the living God*' (2 Ki. 19:16). Poor Sennacherib: it was an unequal contest. 'That night the angel of the Lord went forth, and slew a hundred and eighty-five thousand in the camp of the Assyrians' and, in the exquisitely nonsensical words of the Authorized Version, 'when they arose early in the morning, behold, they were all dead corpses'.

And it is not only His enemies who need to be careful about how they approach the living God. Even for His own people it is an awesome experience. Listen to the amazed reaction to the fire and cloud of Sinai: 'Who is there of all flesh, that has heard the voice of *the living God* speaking out of the midst of the fire, as we have, *and has still lived*?' (Dt. 5:26). And lest we shrug this off as irrelevant in these days of grace, the New Testament also reminds us that 'It is a fearful thing to fall into the hands of the living God' (Heb. 10:31).

But if the God of the Bible makes His real presence felt in awe and terror, this is only one aspect of His character. He is also infinitely desirable. And He gives Himself to those who know and love Him in such a real and personal experience that here again the term 'the living God' comes to the psalmist's lips. The longing of the exile for the 'courts of the Lord' is focused in his desire for a real fellowship with God:

> 'My soul longs, yea, faints
>   for the courts of the Lord;
> my heart and my flesh sing for joy
>   to the living God' (Ps. 84:2).

More poignantly still, Psalm 42 exposes a profound dissatisfaction with anything less than a real personal encounter:

> 'As a hart longs
>   for flowing streams,
> so longs my soul
>   for thee, O God.
> My soul thirsts for God,
>   for the living God.
> When shall I come and behold
>   the face of God?'

If God is in truth 'the living God', then nothing less will do than a living experience of Him, a person-to-person meeting.

The name of God

God has a name. He has many titles, of course, but He also has a name. And names in the Bible are not empty epithets, mere verbal tags for convenience in labelling. They mean something.

God's name is YAHWEH. At least that's what we *think* it is. Because it is so holy, the Hebrews paraphrased it by Adonai, literally 'my Lord', and so in most English versions it appears as 'the LORD'. The vowels of Adonai with the consonants YHWH produced for earlier generations the hybrid 'Jehovah'. No doubt scholars will argue for centuries more about the correct vowels, but for our purposes 'Yahweh' will do.

And God's name has a meaning. It seems to be derived from the Hebrew verb 'to be', or at least from a close relative of it meaning 'to become'. But it was in Moses' encounter with God at the burning bush that it was explained.

Moses was doubtful. He didn't want to act the heroic

deliverer, even after God's assurance, 'But I will be with you'. In any case, who was this God who was sending him to do the impossible? Perhaps he had a vague idea himself, but he knew the sceptical Israelites would not credit it, and he was not theologian enough to answer them. 'If . . . they ask me, "What is his name?" what shall I say to them?'

And God answered him in words which, to us at least, seem to make matters ten times worse. The scholars oscillate from one interpretation to another, and the rest of us resign ourselves to a frustrated ignorance. 'God said to Moses, "I am who I am." And he said, "Say this to the people of Israel, 'I am has sent me to you.' " God also said to Moses, "Say this to the people of Israel, 'Yahweh, the God of your fathers, the God of Abraham, the God of Isaac, and the God of Jacob, has sent me to you' " ' (Ex. 3:14, 15).

'I am', Yahweh, 'I am who I am': what does it all add up to? While the scholars argue as to whether the verb is present or future, simple or causative, one thing is clear: the answer lies in this verb 'to be'. Is God then 'He who is', the static, impassive, absolute being around whom everything revolves? If the language were Greek, that might be the meaning, but it is Hebrew, and in Hebrew the verb 'to be' is dynamic.

Take just one example. You cannot read far in the prophets without meeting the phrase, 'The word of the Lord came to . . .'. But the verb there is the verb 'to be': 'the word of the Lord *was* to . . .'. Ask the prophet concerned, and he will tell you this is no cold metaphysical fact. It is dynamic, uncomfortable, even devastating. When the word of the Lord came to you, you knew about it, and it had an uncanny way of making its presence known in tangible, practical effects. One could paraphrase by, 'The word of the Lord became a living reality to . . .'. 'To be' in Hebrew means an active, dynamic presence.

And this was what Moses needed. Not just the assurance

that God existed, but that He was *there*, present beside him, to carry out His own purpose of deliverance, active, real, dependable. To Moses perhaps the answer meant far more than any English translation can mean to us; it contained reassurance enough for the doubt of Moses and the scepticism of his people. It meant the real presence of the living God.

All this was in answer to the expected query, 'What is His name?' Yahweh, then, is the personal name of the living God, a name to put fresh heart into His people. 'The name Yahweh called up the idea of *the living, awe-inspiring presence of God*.'[2]

And this is our God. He has not changed.

God in human form

It is one of the marks of our departure from the biblical way of thinking about God, as the living God, that we are inclined to be ashamed of anthropomorphism (the description of God as if He were in human form). We pass it off as a rather regrettable primitive phase in the evolution of thinking about God, just a step higher than sheer idolatry, a crude and unsophisticated language which our more advanced and respectable theology has translated into abstract concepts.

While we may not feel too bad about reading that God speaks, hears and sees, we feel decidedly uneasy at the thought of His laughing, smelling, or even whistling![3] But not only does the Old Testament speak of God doing these

---

[2] T. C. Vriezen, *An Outline of Old Testament Theology* (ET, Blackwell), p. 195.
[3] See respectively Gn. 1:3; Ex. 3:7; Gn. 1:4; Ps. 2:4; Gn. 8:21; Is. 5:26, for just one example of each.

things: it also attributes to Him the necessary organs for doing them, mouth, ears, eyes, nostrils, feet, hands and arms.[4] It goes further, and draws vivid pictures of God acting in a very human way: He walks in the garden in the cool of the day (Gn. 3:8), comes down to see what is going on at Babel (Gn. 11:5), and buries Moses with His own hand (Dt. 34:6). He rides on a cherub with clouds as His canopy (Ps. 18:10, 11), gathers the wind in His fists and wraps the waters in His cloak (Pr. 30:4), and sits above the earth, pitching the heavens as His tent (Is. 40:22). Particularly He is a warrior, a man of war, complete with bows and arrows, chariots and horses (Ex. 15:3 and often: see especially the whole imagery of Hab. 3).

Nor is this tendency limited to the actions of God; His feelings are no less human. We are used to the idea of His love, His pity, and even His joy. But expressions of His hatred, disgust, jealousy and repentance do not come so naturally to us.

But all this is not crude, semi-idolatrous thinking. It is just the opposite. It is an expression, the only effective expression, of an intense sense of the real presence and dynamic activity of the living God. It was precisely because they knew God not as a static idol or as a metaphysical theory, but as one to be reckoned with, that they used this forceful imagery. What abstract phraseology could you coin to compare in vivid reality with this?

'Smoke went up from his nostrils,
   and devouring fire from his mouth;
   glowing coals flamed forth from him.
He bowed the heavens, and came down;
   thick darkness was under his feet. . . .

[4] See, *e.g.*, Dt. 8:3; Ps. 34:15; 2 Ch. 16:9; Ex. 15:8; 24:10; Ps. 119:73; Is. 51:9.

He reached from on high, he took me,
> he drew me out of many waters' (Ps. 18:8, 9, 16).

Indeed, is it not true that the better we know God, in experience as well as in theory, the more meaningful and precious such language becomes to us still? Is it an accident that we still use such phrases as 'walking with God' to convey a depth of spiritual experience which is far removed from primitive idolatry? To the men of the Old Testament God was *real*. They *knew* Him. And the clearest way they could express it was in the language of human personality and activity, not in cold metaphysical jargon. All honour to them! If we knew God better, we might find our tidy theological formulations less than adequate. God has a way of breaking loose.

God as a person

One question raised by the debate around *Honest to God* has been whether it is right to speak of God as 'a person' or even as 'personal'. These are not, of course, biblical terms: the Bible is not given to such abstractions. But the question is important. For much of our language about God uses personal categories, and if, as some modern theologians are insisting, there is no 'person' to whom such language applies, but only a principle, the Ground of Being, or some such intangible idea, then the honesty of using it at all becomes questionable. If it cannot be 'cashed', it has no value.

A 'person' is not easily defined. The following outline, though it would not pass muster in a dictionary, captures roughly what I mean by the term. A person is a conscious being, one who thinks, feels, and purposes, and carries these purposes into action, one too who has active relationships with others – you can talk to a person, and get a response;

you can share feelings and ideas with him, argue with him, love him, hate him; you can *know* him, in a way which can only be described as 'personal'!

If this understanding of the term 'person' is anywhere near what other people mean by it, then there is no doubt at all that the Bible sees God as 'a person'.[5] God thinks and plans, loves and hates, is grieved and pleased, purposes and fulfils His purpose. He acts, in a practical, discernible way. The whole Bible is about His acting, not only through other persons (a principle *could* be said to do that), but directly, on His own. And God is one with whom real relationships can be established. Communion with God is a real and personal thing. Men pray, and He answers; they love Him, hate Him, reject Him; they share His love, His joy, and His concern. Above all, they *know* Him, as we shall see in the third chapter. The Old Testament uses the same verb for 'knowing' God as it uses for the relationship of man and woman at its most intimate. If your wife can be an abstract, impersonal principle, then so can God!

God and idols

Whatever may be said of the God of the Bible, it can hardly be that He is nebulous and irrelevant. He has a way of breaking decisively into people's lives, meeting doubt with tangible proof, and hostility with devastating power, and establishing a relationship with men which both terrifies them and leaves them longing for more.

He is not an academic proposition. The Bible provides us with no definition of the word 'God' – it cannot, because, as Pascal said, 'Dieu défini, c'est Dieu fini'. A God who is susceptible to the static delineation of cold philosophy, or

[5] This is not, of course, to deny the Christian doctrine of *three* Persons in one substance: that is a quite distinct technical use of the term.

even of a rigid dogmatic theology, is not the dynamic God of the Bible. God is known by His words and His acts, not by abstract speculation. To try to tie Him down with human definitions is idolatry; and it is idolatry which draws out some of the most superbly scathing mockery of the Old Testament.

An idol is a lifeless image. It cannot *do* anything. Therefore it is dead: it cannot be a god, because gods are alive and active. Read the gentler mockery of Psalms 115:3-8 and 135:15-18; then turn to Isaiah, the scourge of the idols.

'To whom then will you liken God,
  or what likeness compare with him?
The idol! a workman casts it,
  and a goldsmith overlays it with gold,
  and casts for it silver chains.
He who is impoverished chooses for an offering
  wood that will not rot;
he seeks out a skilful craftsman
  to set up an image that will not move.
Have you not known? . . .'

and the prophet goes on to depict in a few deft strokes the God who made the earth and everything in it, who governs the stars in heaven and the nations on earth, and whose power and concern reach down to the weakest of His servants (Is. 40:18ff.; see also 46:5-7). Turn to Isaiah 44, and you will find the most scathing tirade of them all, so that thousands of years later you can still detect the searing sarcasm of his words, and cringe under their scorching impact.

But it is left to Jeremiah (10:1-10) to make the point crystal clear.

'Their idols are like scarecrows in a cucumber field,
  and they cannot speak;

they have to be carried,
   for they cannot walk.
Be not afraid of them,
   for they cannot do evil,
   neither is it in them to do good . . . .
But the Lord is the true God;
   he is *the living God* and the everlasting King.
At his wrath the earth quakes,
   and the nations cannot endure his indignation.'

An idol can do nothing; therefore it *is* nothing. But God is the living God, and His acts prove it. *He* is to be feared.

God, then, is not to be confined in spatial limits. He is moving, dynamic. If an image is therefore unthinkable, even a static temple is not above reproach, and David's proposal to build one is rejected. 'Would you build me a house to dwell in? I have not dwelt in a house since the day I brought up the people of Israel from Egypt to this day, but I have been moving about in a tent for my dwelling' (2 Sa. 7: 5, 6). Stephen and Paul take up the refrain (Acts 7:44-50; 17:24-29). God cannot be confined. He is too big, too dynamic, for any human limits.

But still we have not learned it. Men still try to confine God to the limits of *their* reason and imagination, if not in physical images and temples. Because a God so confined is nicely in their power: He can be controlled. They confine Him in temples of metaphysical philosophy and images of systematic theology, and they take no account of the living God, who 'does not live in shrines made by man' (Acts 17:24). Our modern idolatry is no less disastrous than that of Canaan. It gives us an abstract God who can *do* nothing, whom there is no cause to fear, who is dead. And it leaves us cosily unaware of the living God.

The living God in the New Testament

In the New Testament, literal idols are not the only focus of false religion. They are there, indeed, and the same contrast is drawn as in the Old Testament. The Thessalonians 'turned to God from idols, to serve a *living* and true God' (1 Thes. 1:9), and Paul and Barnabas, hailed as Hermes and Zeus by the Lycaonians, begged them to 'turn from these vain things to a *living God* who made the heaven and the earth and the sea and all that is in them' (Acts 14:15). Paul's address to the Areopagus, provoked by the idolatry of the Athenians, has the same thrust (Acts 17:22-31).

But the Letter to the Hebrews in particular makes use of the term 'the living God' to combat not idolatry but a dead and formal religion, however pure and spiritual its belief in the one true God. It was written to a group of Jewish Christians who were wavering in their new faith, and contemplating a return to Judaism, with all its rites and ceremonies, its laws and traditions. The writer is staggered. This would be to 'fall away from the living God' (3:12). Christ did not come to perpetuate a formal religion: He died to 'purify your conscience from dead works to serve the living God' (9:14). Think of the privilege of it: the Israelites at Sinai received God's law in mystery and terror, hedged in by prohibitions and dire warnings, 'but you have come to Mount Zion and to the city of the living God . . .' (12:22). To throw all that away, and return to a frustrating, ineffective rigmarole of 'dead works', would be not only mad, but dangerous: 'It is a fearful thing to fall into the hands of the living God' (10:31).

Many speak today of the 'abolition of religion', and of 'religionless Christianity'. If by 'religion' they mean the substitution of a scheme of doctrine and ethics and ceremonial for a living relationship with the living God, then the Letter to the Hebrews said it long before them, and the whole Bible would echo 'Amen'.

A living relationship with the living God. That is Christianity; that is the heart of true religion. Christians are 'the temple of the living God' (2 Cor. 6:16), their very life derived through Christ from 'the living Father' (Jn. 6:57; cf. 5:26), and the undeniable reality of the change in their lives witnessing to the work of 'the Spirit of the living God' in them (2 Cor. 3:3); they press on undaunted by opposition and discouragement, because they have their 'hope set on the living God' (1 Tim. 4:10), and because He is the living God their hope is not disappointed. These few uses of the term 'the living God' are some visible outcrops of a stratum running richly through the whole of the New Testament, the conviction that God not only 'is', but 'lives', in dynamic and irresistible power, and in such a person-to-person relationship with His people that there is no room for idolatry or formal 'religion'.

When a small ghetto of undistinguished men and women, fresh from a taste of the displeasure of the authorities and confronted by a complete ban on preaching, could voice a prayer like the following, what was the secret of it? 'Now, Lord, look upon their threats, and grant to thy servants to speak thy word with all boldness, while thou stretchest out thy hand to heal, and signs and wonders are performed through the name of thy holy servant Jesus.' And they meant every word of it; subsequent history shows that! 'And when they had prayed, the place in which they were gathered together was shaken; and they were all filled with the Holy Spirit and spoke the word of God with boldness' (Acts 4:29-31). No wonder, if they could say a prayer like that! Is not this belief in the living God?

Read on through Acts, and see the reality of the living God set out for all to see, in the dynamic power of the Holy Spirit, the explosive, world-subverting crusade of men and women who believed in a God who acts, directly, effectively, right down in the human situation, be it in prison or palace. Watch the hand of this living God intervening, in answer to His people's prayer, working miracles, converting thousands, opening prison doors, and raising the dead, guiding His messengers to people and places they had never thought of, supervising the whole operation and every figure in it so as to work out His purpose in the end. Is it any wonder they prayed, constantly, not in vague generalities, but in daring specific requests? To them, God was real; to them He was the living God.

The living God and the church

It is this view of God as the living God which the present-day Christian church, at least in those Western lands which it still fondly regards as the Christian nations, has lost sight of. Even those parts of the church which profess to take the Bible seriously, while they pay lip-service to its teaching, know little of the living God in practice and in experience. And so the church stagnates. It has lost its driving force. It becomes a museum for the preservation of hallowed traditions and institutions, doctrines and sentiment. But it has no life.

In despair, theologians have tried to come to terms with the situation by accepting it and formulating a theology to justify it. They have reduced God to a vague, impersonal idea, a symbol of ultimate concern, or an ethical sanction, or they have dispensed with Him altogether. Anything to escape the crude dynamism of the biblical teaching, which contrasts so uncomfortably and mockingly with our sophisticated lifelessness.

They could not have done it if Christians had been true to their calling, if the reality of the living God had been inescapably evident on every street corner, as His people took Him at His word, and proved His power. To have said that God was dead in the presence of Paul and the churches of his day would have been ludicrous.

We may point the finger at old-fashioned liberal theology, with its rejection of the supernatural and reduction of Christianity to the commonplace, to explain the absurd utterances of some modern theologians. But no less blame attaches to those of us who have held to the form of a biblical religion, with its doctrine of a personal and dynamic God, but by our lives have denied, or at least never known, the power of it. And it may be that the answer to the current rejection or watering-down of God, and the consequent secularization of Christianity, lies not so much in apologetic or polemic speech and writing as in the rediscovery, in terms of practical day-to-day living, of a biblical knowledge of the living God.

2 KNOWING ABOUT GOD

Psalm 14 introduces us to the fool, who says in his heart, 'There is no God' (Ps. 14:1; *cf.* 10:4). He is an oddity, because the Bible knows no atheists.

But even he is not an atheist, as we understand the term. For the same fool who says 'There is no God' thinks a few verses later, 'God has forgotten, he has hidden his face, he will never see it' (Ps. 10:4, 11). There is no God, and He has forgotten! It reminds one of the cynical formulation of the creed of the death-of-God theologians: 'There is no God, and Jesus is His Son.'

The only atheism the Bible knows is not speculative, but practical. If God has no impact on my life, if He is not a force to be reckoned with, if He is not a God who acts, then in practical terms 'there is no God'. Such was the fool's reasoning. The bare existence of God is not the question, but His relevance. If I can ignore Him, even flout Him, and get away with it, He doesn't count: 'There is no God.'

The fool in the Old Testament is in fact as much knave as fool. The Hebrew word for it is *nabal*, and the story of one owner of that name gives an insight into its meaning (see 1 Sa. 25). Psalm 14, where we meet this 'fool', is not in fact about bad theology, but about bad living. That is biblical atheism, to ignore and flout God, not to deny His existence.

His existence is in fact self-evident. The biblical writers neither argue it nor defend it. They assume it. The living presence of God is an axiom of biblical thought. He imposes Himself on men's minds. He is inescapably real and present. The Bible knows idolaters, worshippers of other gods, backsliders, and rebels; but it knows no atheists.

The traditional 'proofs of the existence of God' find no echo in biblical thinking. They were not needed. The Bible does in fact direct our attention to the revelation of God in nature, but not to prove His existence. Nature can teach us much about a God already known; it cannot by itself prove that He exists. But of this we shall have more to say shortly. The point here is that the Bible does not concern itself with existence, but with life. The big question is whether God is the living God, and that is a practical question. It is answered not by philosophical reasoning, but in personal experience. The question of the existence of God gives way to that of the knowledge of God.

Natural theology

Modern scientific man gains his knowledge by observation and deduction. He examines the phenomena of the world around him, its structure and its working; he investigates his own make-up, and the movement of human affairs; and he then draws conclusions which are the basic raw materials of scientific knowledge. It is not surprising that he hopes, or rather used to hope, to take a similar road to the knowledge of God. It was only natural.

'Natural theology', it was called. Nowadays almost all Protestant theologians reject it in principle as a route to the knowledge of God, but it has a tendency to creep in by the back door in practice. For the only real alternative is supernatural revelation, and that is still less popular!

What is the status of natural theology? Or, to put it in basic English, can God be known by man's unaided observation and reason? The biblical position would seem to be that observation of the created world and its workings can, indeed should, tell us much about its Creator, but cannot by itself lead us to the knowledge of God in the full biblical sense.[1] Rather its function is to increase our understanding of a God already known to us by other means, and to lead us to a fuller dependence and worship.

Thus baldly stated, this might seem a cold and academic subject. But biblical thought is seldom open to that accusation, even though our modern attempts to systematize it may be. We turn now to some of the biblical passages which raise this question of the revelation of God in the created order, and particularly in the three spheres of nature, man, and history.

Nature

Natural revelation in the Old Testament

'The heavens are telling the glory of God;
    and the firmament proclaims his handiwork.
Day to day pours forth speech,
    and night to night declares knowledge.
There is no speech, nor are there words;
    their voice is not heard;
yet their voice goes out through all the earth,
    and their words to the end of the world'

(Ps. 19:1–4).

The movement of the sun through the heavens, from end to end, shedding its warmth over the whole world, is a word-

---

[1] We shall examine this biblical sense in the next chapter; for the moment let it be noted that by 'knowledge of God' we mean something personal, a matter of relationship rather than of theory.

less revelation of the glory and power and wisdom of the One who made it with His own hands. But that is not the end of the Psalm, and it goes on to speak in still more glowing terms of the law, the testimony, the precepts, the commandments and the ordinances of the Lord. It is these that revive the soul, make the simple wise, rejoice the heart, and enlighten the eyes (verses 7-10).

> 'More to be desired are they than gold,
>   even much fine gold;
> sweeter also than honey
>   and drippings of the honeycomb.'

There is a warning here: the forthright declaration that God reveals Himself to man through nature is balanced by a far higher eulogy of His revelation of Himself through His words. It is these that are the guide to right living and a true relationship with God (verses 11-14).

But natural revelation still has its place, and a very high one. To look at the natural order of the world is, for the man of God, to be moved to a new appreciation of the greatness and wisdom of the Creator.

> 'Bless the Lord, O my soul!
> O Lord my God, thou art very great!
> Thou art clothed with honour and majesty',

and Psalm 104 goes on to describe God's creation of the world, the intricate balance and design of the whole operation, and the way He not only made it all, but still controls and sustains all its movements, and all the creatures in it from the badgers in the rocks to Leviathan sporting in the sea.

> 'O Lord, how manifold are thy works!
> In wisdom hast thou made them all' (verse 24).

Day by day they look to Him for all they need, storks, goats, badgers, lions, Leviathan, yes, and even man himself:

'When thou openest thy hand, they are filled with
    good things.
When thy hidest thy face, they are dismayed;
    when thou takest away their breath, they die
    and return to their dust' (verses 28, 29).

Faced with such undeniable majesty, glory, and wisdom,
the psalmist can only resolve, and delights to resolve,

'I will sing to the Lord as long as I live;
    I will sing praise to my God while I have being.'

Such a revelation of the greatness of God may be very
much needed. Isaiah was writing for a people in despair,
who thought God had forgotten and abandoned them (Is.
40:27). His answer is to point to God's creation, the immensity and the precision of it (verses 12ff.). Particularly, he
points to the stars:

'Lift up your eyes on high and see:
    who created these?
He who brings out their host by number,
    calling them all by name;
by the greatness of his might,
    and because he is strong in power
    not one is missing' (verse 26).

In contrast to such a God, idols are laughable, and the
strongest human rulers are like stubble. Can *such* a God forget His own people, or fail to help them in their need?

'Have you not known? Have you not heard?
The Lord is the everlasting God,
    the Creator of the ends of the earth.
He does not faint or grow weary,
    his understanding is unsearchable.

He gives power to the faint,
and to him who has no might he increases strength'
(verses 28, 29).

The chronic affliction of God's people, no less than of other men, is their tendency to belittle God. Their God is too small. If only they would use their eyes, and look at the world around them, they would see ample evidence of His greatness, and of His incredible wisdom and care in the smallest detail as well as in the master-plan as a whole. They would not dare to distrust Him again.

This was what Job needed to learn. He believed in the goodness and justice of God, though the intensity of his suffering made even that belief waver at times. But he had no conception of the greatness and wisdom of God. He tried to peg Him down to his own finite standards of fair play. Let none of us blame Job. We would have come through the test no better. But the fact remains that his God was too small, and he wanted to keep Him that way. And it was this situation that drew out the most superb panorama of the wonder of God's creation to be found in the whole Bible. For four whole chapters (38-41) the majestic pageant passes by, earth and sea, light and darkness, snow, hail, wind and rain, stars, storms, and clouds; then lions, ravens, goats and deer, the wild ass, the ostrich, the war-horse, and the hawk, each more wonderful than the last; finally that fearsome monster, Behemoth, the hippopotamus, and his even more terrible playmate, Leviathan, the crocodile. And there the awesome catalogue comes to an abrupt halt. God has no need to draw the moral, and Job has no more to say.

'I had heard of thee by the hearing of the ear,
but now my eye sees thee;
therefore I despise myself,
and repent in dust and ashes' (42:5, 6).

What else could he do? You cannot question the wisdom of a God like that, or accuse Him of not playing the game. So Job's story has a happy ending.

Natural revelation in the New Testament

The Old Testament, then, would tell us to look at the world around us if we want to gain at least a glimpse of the greatness, the power, the wisdom, and the glory of the God who created it and sustains it. We have looked at a few outstanding examples of this; there are plenty more.

The New Testament agrees. Paul chides the idolatrous Lycaonians for not realizing what God is like, 'a living God who made the heaven and the earth and the sea and all that is in them'. They had no special verbal revelation from God, 'yet he did not leave himself without witness, for he did good and gave you from heaven rains and fruitful seasons, satisfying your hearts with food and gladness' (Acts 14:15-17). In nature alone they had enough data to tell them something of God, enough to make them see the folly of idolatry.

This, too, is the point of Paul's much-discussed address to the Areopagus at Athens (Acts 17:22-31). The Greeks had reduced God to lifeless idols and man-made shrines. Paul's rebuke is essentially that they should have known better. God made the world and everything in it; He is the source of life and breath and everything; He organized man's life on earth 'that they should seek God, in the hope that they might feel after him and find him'. He is near to every man; indeed man is His 'offspring'. 'Being then God's offspring, we ought not to think that the Deity is like gold, or silver, or stone, a representation by the art and imagination of man.' They ought to have known, even without a special revelation from God. The world and everything in it, including man himself, should have told them.

But, as in Psalm 19, the address does not end there, but turns to the fuller revelation of God's will in the sending of

Jesus. Their previous ignorance could be overlooked: now they are without excuse.

These addresses were designed for particular occasions and particular audiences. For the full theological treatment of this theme we must turn to the first chapter of Romans. Without indulging in a full exposition and discussion of Paul's thinking, we may notice how what was implicit in the addresses in Acts here comes into the full light of day. God's judgment of men is not because they are ignorant, but because they suppress the truth which they cannot evade. 'For what can be known about God is plain to them, because God has shown it to them. Ever since the creation of the world his invisible nature, namely, his eternal power and deity, has been clearly perceived in the things that have been made. So they are without excuse' (Rom. 1:19, 20).

It could hardly be put more bluntly than that. There *is* a natural revelation of God in His creation. So plain is it, indeed, that Paul does not simply say that they should have known better, but that they *did* know better, and deliberately rejected that knowledge: 'they exchanged the truth about God for a lie', 'they did not see fit to acknowledge God' (verses 25, 28). We are back to the fool of Psalm 10, who recognized God's existence, but refused to take Him into account. Paul actually goes so far as to say that they 'knew God', though it is obvious from the sequel that he is using 'know' here in a lower sense than is usual in the Bible, as we shall see later.

Notice that what Paul specifies as being clear about God from creation is 'his eternal power and deity'. This amounts to the same as we saw in the Old Testament passages above, the majesty, power, and glory of God. 'Deity' could be paraphrased as 'that which shows God to be God, and gives Him the right to worship':[2] it means His majesty, His

---

[2] So H. Kleinknecht in *Theological Dictionary of the New Testament* (Eerdmans), edited by G. Kittel, vol. III, p. 123.

transcendence, His holiness. Literally, it is simply His 'God-ness'.

It may be worth pointing out in passing that Romans 2:12-16, which is sometimes quoted as teaching that the 'good pagan' is really a worshipper of God and does not need any further revelation, does not in fact teach this at all, but simply states that there is a natural moral awareness by which those who have no written law may be judged. Its purpose in context is to point out that, since no-one lives up even to that standard, none is exempt from the general condemnation which is the terrible conclusion of chapters 1-3. Thus this passage says nothing on the question of a natural revelation of God.

The limits of natural revelation
There is, then, enough in the created world to tell man something of the nature of God, His greatness, power, and wisdom, enough to put idolatry, or any other devaluing of God, out of court. Even without any other revelation, man ought to reverence and worship the God who made the earth and everything in it.

But that is only one side of the biblical evidence. There is a further sense in which it is impossible for man, unaided, to come to a true knowledge of God. Paul discusses this point particularly in 1 Corinthians 2, the burden of which is that human wisdom could never discover the wisdom of God, which is revealed only by the Spirit of God to those who possess the Spirit. There is a point beyond which 'the natural man' cannot go, and knowledge of God, in the full meaning of that term, lies beyond that point. However correct a picture of God his observation of the world may lead him to (and there is a limit to that too), it can never bring him into that spiritual relationship with God which is real knowledge, as the Bible understands the term. And without such knowledge, the whole question is really an academic one.

What then is the status of natural theology in the Bible? Firstly, it has nothing to do with proving the *existence* of God. This is not a biblical question. There is nothing in the Bible remotely resembling the cosmological and teleological proofs of scholastic philosophy. God is simply *there*, and this is the axiomatic starting-point of biblical thought. The Bible does not even attempt to prove that it was He who created the world; it simply states it. It is a matter of faith (Heb. 11:3) not discerned by scientific observation. Thus the Bible gives no warrant for telling an atheist to look at the world around him, and then chiding him for not believing in God. What it does suggest is that we can rightly tell a *theist* to look at the world, and chide him for having too low an idea of the God he believes in, for denying His almighty power and transcendence, or His wisdom and care.

But the sort of understanding of God which can be achieved by simple observation of the world is only rudimentary. It does not lead to a true *knowledge* of God; that is achieved by other means, as we shall see shortly. But when it *is* achieved, then natural revelation comes into its own. For it is the man who knows God who can then turn to the world around him and learn about the God he knows. Now he has a point of reference, and what was previously an obscure and confusing revelation becomes an open book. He can look at a world created and sustained by the God he now knows, and can sing with the Psalmist, 'O Lord my God, thou art very great!'

It boils down to this: you cannot expect an atheist to reach a personal knowledge of God through looking at nature; but you *can* expect a Christian's observation of nature to lead him to worship with greater understanding and reverence the God who has revealed Himself to him.

This conclusion will be seen to apply equally to the other two areas of natural revelation which we singled out, namely man and history; these can be more briefly dealt with.

Man

'So God created man in his own image, in the image of God he created him' (Gn. 1:27). And if man is created in the image of God, surely here is a safe route to the knowledge of God. Cannot God be known by the study of His image?

To get this whole question in perspective, it is worth pointing out that the idea of man as made in the image of God occurs only in three passages in Genesis 1-9, and in two incidental references in the New Testament.[3] It is not therefore unimportant, but the scarcity of its occurrence would be strange if the idea were in fact used as a key to learning about God.

In fact it is never so used. Without entering into what is a very complicated discussion, we may safely say that the image of God is what distinguishes man from the animals, giving him a unique dignity in the created order. It is probably to be seen as embracing his personality, his rationality, and his capacity for a spiritual relationship with God. And its use in each biblical occurrence is to demonstrate the high dignity of man, as being in a sense in the same bracket as God, over against the animal creation.

But can one then look at man and from him learn about God? We have seen how God is described in vividly human terms, and this would seem to suggest that the nature of man may teach us something of the nature of God. But such an argument is superficial. How else *could* God reveal Himself to man? Indeed, how can man grasp anything except in terms drawn from his own experience, from his own world? Any language about God is bound to use analogy.

[3] 1 Cor. 11:7; Jas. 3:9. These are the only New Testament uses of the term applying it to mankind as a whole, rather than to Christians, or more particularly to Christ Himself.

It is quite true that man forms a very useful, indeed necessary, analogy for the understanding of God, and that God intended it should be so. But God's use of man as an analogy for the communication of truth about Himself should not lead man to believe that he can perceive such analogies unaided. One cannot single out any given aspect of man, even man at his best, and claim that it follows that God must be like that too. This is something the Bible does not do. Its result would be idolatry.

Man is, of course, a part of God's creation. As such, the wonder of his make-up constitutes a testimony to the wisdom and power of his Creator (see, e.g., Ps. 139:13-18). In this sense man is indeed a datum for the knowledge of God. But this is a position he shares with the rest of creation. And this is the only biblical sense in which one can look at man and learn about God.

All this could have been left unsaid if it were not for the tendency of certain modern theologians to do what the Bible does not do: to tell man to look into himself and there find God. Dr J. A. T. Robinson, the former Bishop of Woolwich, is by no means alone in suggesting that when you have delved into the very core of your being, and found that which is of ultimate significance to you, you have found God. The Archbishop of Canterbury has pronounced as follows:

'We need to see if there are some who are helped by thinking not about God above us in heaven, or even God around and near, but about the deep-down meaning of human life in terms of love. There may be those who find there the heart of the matter; and this *is* God, even though a man may not be able to cry with Thomas, "My Lord and my God".'[4]

But according to the Bible this is not even the way to begin to look for God. While God is the source of all that is

[4] A. M. Ramsey, *Image Old and New* (SPCK), p. 14.

good in us, He is not contained in it, any more than He is contained in the rest of His creation. Man as a part of creation has his place as a datum in natural theology, but it is no more exalted than that of the rest of the natural order. God's definitive revelation of Himself comes from elsewhere.

History

God controls what goes on in His world, and this includes the events of human history. Not only His own people, but all nations come under His direction.

> 'Did I not bring up Israel from the land of Egypt,
> *and* the Philistines from Caphtor and the Syrians from
>   Kir?' (Am. 9:7).

Surely here, in the majestic movements of world history, and particularly in God's dealings with His own people, we may expect to find something of His nature writ large.

But again the answer must be the same as for His revelation in nature. There is indeed a revelation of God in history, but it is not complete in itself. Israel constantly drew lessons from God's acts in their history, and particularly the Exodus. The magnificent hymn of Moses after the crossing of the Red Sea (Ex. 15:1-18) is the first and finest example of this. The glorious triumph of Yahweh over Pharaoh and his chariots reveals Him as a 'man of war', and displays His power, His majesty, and His steadfast love for His people.

> 'Who is like thee, O Lord, among the gods?
>   Who is like thee, majestic in holiness,
>   terrible in glorious deeds, doing wonders?
> Thou didst stretch out thy right hand,
>   the earth swallowed them' (Ex. 15:11, 12).

But what if there had been no Moses, no prophets, to interpret the acts of God? Are they an open book for all to read? Would a simple, unbiased observation of human history, with all its wars, its atrocities, and its disasters, lead to a true understanding of the nature of God? He would be a supreme optimist who thought so.

It has been fashionable to speak of God as revealed in acts and not in words. This is a complete reversal of the biblical viewpoint. For God made sure that when a significant event occurred there was a prophet at hand to interpret it: Moses for the Exodus, Jeremiah and Ezekiel for the Exile, Isaiah for the return of the exiles, and the apostles and evangelists for the life and death of Jesus and the growth of the early church, to name but a few.

If there had been no Moses, the Exodus could have been just another tribal migration. Without Jeremiah and Ezekiel, who would ever have seen in the Exile anything more than the inevitable onward march of Babylon? And as for the return from the Exile, without the magnificent interpretation of Isaiah 40 ff. it would be the greatest non-event of Israelite history!

It is not simply that without these men we would have known little of the bare history, though this is true. But its significance, its theological aspect, would have been completely lost. And without that, where is the revelation? 'The events of history as such do not themselves constitute a revelation; it is the prophetic interpretation . . . which is the vehicle of special revelation. . . . Where there are no prophets, there can be no special revelation.'[5] Or, as Amos put it more succinctly,

'Surely the Lord God does nothing,
without revealing his secret
to his servants the prophets' (Am. 3:7).

[5] A. Richardson, *Christian Apologetics* (SCM Press), pp. 140-141.

Act without word, therefore, is empty as a vehicle of revelation. History could tell us whatever we wanted to read from it, if God left it without an interpreter.

God's initiative

Our estimate of natural theology, as the Bible sees it, thus boils down to this. Man's observation of nature, of man and of history can never lead him to the knowledge of God, in more than a superficial intellectual sense, and even this is limited. Given a belief in the existence of God, he may find from these sources some indication of what that God is like. Given a true personal knowledge of God, he may learn to trust and worship his God more fully, and with a greater understanding, from seeing the work of His hands. But to gain his initial belief in the existence of God, and still more to gain any true personal knowledge of God, he will have to turn elsewhere.

This means that man cannot be the final arbiter. It is not within his power to find God unaided. The initiative is with God. One would have thought that this would be obvious, if God is transcendent and man is His creature, but human self-confidence dies hard, and man will always try by himself to 'find out the deep things of God' and 'the limit of the Almighty' (Jb. 11:7). But the Bible gives him no encouragement. 'The secret things belong to the Lord our God; but the things that are revealed belong to us' (Dt. 29:29). God reserves the right to reveal what He will and how He will. The amazing and marvellous thing is that He has done so, and in a manner which puts the wildest claims of natural theology in the shade.

But that deserves another chapter.

3 KNOWING GOD

If God is to be known by man, it will be on God's terms, and in God's chosen way. It is He who must take the initiative. This was the conclusion of our last chapter; indeed one might almost claim that it is plain common sense, on any but a pathetically inadequate understanding of the nature of God.

And God has chosen to communicate with man by His word. For God is not only the God who acts, but the God who speaks. Creation began with a word of God (Gn. 1:3), and from the first creation of man God declared His will to him by a word (Gn. 1:28; 2:16, *etc.*). It would be an impossible labour to count the number of times the Bible records that 'God said . . .', 'God spoke . . .', 'God commanded . . .'; nor is it necessary, for no reader of the Bible can fail to perceive that if God is characterized by dynamic activity, He is no less constantly represented as revealing His nature and His will by word of mouth.

But there is not so much difference between God's action and His speaking as we might think. To the modern Western mind, 'word' signifies a tool of verbal communication, the vehicle by which thoughts are conveyed from speaker to hearer. Thus it can meaningfully be opposed to 'act'. Not so for the Hebrew mind of the Old Testament. For them, a word was something active, dynamic, almost concrete. Indeed, the same Hebrew word means both 'word' and 'thing'.

Take Isaac's blessing, for example (Gn. 27). He gave it to the wrong person. Now we would say, 'What's in a word? After all, it was uttered in ignorance, stolen by deceit. Let him declare it null and void.' But a Hebrew could not say that. The word had gone out, and it was irrevocable. And with that word went the blessing itself. Now it was gone, lost for ever, and there was no more to be given to Esau.

> 'We may perhaps most easily envisage how the Hebrews thought that the word spoken with intent could have effect by recalling the manner in which characters are made to speak in a modern newspaper comic strip. There the words of the actors are ringed around and connected by a line to the speaker's mouth. Their words have a very solid and objective look about them. Before they were uttered, the words were hidden in the speaker's heart. But now that they are clearly enunciated, they have become an object, a thing, and are separate from the person who uttered them; yet they express the speaker's heart or purpose. However, it has now become impossible to push the words back into the speaker's mouth. There they stand, uttered and out, and are so potent in themselves that in the next picture frame we are shown their effect upon the other characters in the comic strip.'[1]

And so it is with the word of God.

> 'By myself I have sworn,
>   from my mouth has gone forth in righteousness
>   a word that shall not return:
> "To me every knee shall bow,
>   every tongue shall swear" ' (Is. 45:23).

[1] G. A. F. Knight, *A Christian Theology of the Old Testament* (SCM Press), p. 56.

The word has gone out, and so now the thing is sure. It only remains to await its inevitable effect.

'So shall my word be that goes forth from my mouth;
    it shall not return to me empty,
but it shall accomplish that which I purpose,
    and prosper in the thing for which I sent it'
(Is. 55:11; cf. 31:2).

So the word is an independent, dynamic agent. God's word does not simply convey His will, but accomplishes it. The word of God is like a fire, and a hammer that shatters the rock (Je. 23:29). He 'sends it forth' to bring deliverance to His people (Ps. 107:20), and it 'runs swiftly' through the earth to accomplish His purpose in the world of nature (Ps. 145:15, 18). Indeed, it was by His word that the whole universe was created (Ps. 33:6, 9; <i>cf.</i> Gn. 1:3, <i>etc.</i>). Perhaps most vividly of all, Isaiah warns the rebellious nation that

'The Lord has sent a word against Jacob,
    and it will light upon (literally "fall into") Israel'
(Is. 9:8).

'It is like a projectile shot into the enemy camp, whose explosion must sometimes be awaited but which is always inevitable, and these explosions are the events of history.'[2]

And this is the word by which God has communicated with man. This is the word which 'came to' the prophets and men of God, from Genesis 15:1 right through the Old Testament. It was not usually a comfortable experience: indeed it could be quite shattering. Jeremiah in particular went through agony as this dynamic word possessed him. It led him into reproach and derision, and he decided he had had enough; he would prophesy no more (Je. 20:7-9). But

---

[2] E. Jacob, *Theology of the Old Testament* (ET, Hodder and Stoughton), p. 131.

he had not reckoned with the power of the word:

> 'There is in my heart as it were a burning fire
>   shut up in my bones,
> and I am weary with holding it in,
>   and I cannot.'

When God's word first came to Ezekiel in a vision of terrifying splendour, it left him unable to do anything but sit 'overwhelmed' (literally 'showing terror') for a whole week (Ezk. 3:15). But, as Amos observed, they had no choice:

> 'The lion has roared;
>   who will not fear?
> The Lord God has spoken;
>   who can but prophesy?' (Am. 3:8).

All this makes it very clear that when the Old Testament speaks of the word of the Lord coming to a prophet, it is not a poetic way of saying that he had god-like thoughts. It is saying that an irresistible agency from outside the man gripped him and directed his utterance, that 'no prophecy ever came by the impulse of man, but men moved by the Holy Spirit spoke from God' (2 Pet. 1:21). The whole Bible would repudiate fiercely the idea that its utterances are men's ideas about God: they are the words God gave to them. 'I have put my words in your mouth', said God to Jeremiah (1:9); and Ezekiel was given a scroll of writing to eat, and told, 'Eat this scroll, and go, speak to the house of Israel' (Ezk. 2:8-3:3; *cf.* Rev. 10:8-11). There *were* prophets who uttered their own ideas and 'visions of their own minds', but they were *ipso facto* condemned as false prophets, and in the strongest of terms (Je. 23:16-32). The true prophet might have to wait a long time for the word of God to come (Je. 42:7; Hab. 2:1); he could not invent it.

It is indeed true that the Bible does not countenance a

rigid theory of inspiration by simple 'dictation', and displays clearly the individuality of the prophets and writers in the way their message is expressed and delivered. But it is also unequivocally clear that what is spoken and written is that which God wishes to be spoken and written, and nothing less. The initiative, and the outcome, are God's and His alone.

Moses and Aaron afford a useful illustration. Moses was the leader, but he was not eloquent and so Aaron became his spokesman. 'You shall speak to him and put the words in his mouth. . . . He shall speak for you to the people; and he shall be a mouth for you, and you shall be to him as God. . . . I make you as God to Pharaoh; and Aaron your brother shall be your prophet' (Ex. 4:15, 16; 7:1). As Aaron was Moses' 'mouth', so the prophet is the 'mouth' of God (cf. Je. 15:19). The expression and the rhetorical form are the prophet's, but the message, the effective word, is God's.

The word, then, is the principal means (though by no means the only one) by which God communicated Himself and His will to man in Old Testament days. 'In many and various ways God spoke of old to our fathers by the prophets' (Heb. 1:1). But that is not the end of the sentence.

The word made flesh

If in the Old Testament the word of God was objectified and regarded as a 'thing', indeed almost as an independent agent, the New Testament witnesses to the ultimate development of this process. 'The Word became flesh and dwelt among us' (Jn. 1:14). The word in the Old Testament was an expression of the mind and will, indeed the personality of God. It 'went forth' and conveyed God to men. Now Jesus, as the word made flesh, is a thoroughly concrete embodiment of the very nature of God. He is a living anthropomorphism, God expressed in human form. 'For in him the whole fullness of deity dwells *bodily*' (Col. 2:9). God in a human body, the invisible, spiritual God expressed in visible, physical terms. This is the ultimate anthropomorphism, the human body and its actions used not now as a pictorial image for the activity of God, but as a concrete vehicle of God Himself.

This is the incredible fact with which the New Testament writers struggle to come to terms. There is an awe and an amazement about the way they relate their experience: 'That which was from the beginning, which we have heard, which we have seen with our eyes, which we have looked upon and touched with our hands, concerning the word of life – the life was made manifest, and we saw it, and testify to it, and proclaim to you the eternal life which was with the Father and was made manifest to us . . .' (1 Jn. 1:1, 2). Syntax and style give way before the excited rush of words as John tries to convey the greatest privilege man has known. We actually touched Him!

This is the climax of God's revelation: He has actually become visible. 'No one has ever seen God; the only-begotten God (for so the text most probably reads), who is in the bosom of the Father, he has made him known' (Jn. 1:18). No-one has seen God – He is invisible; and yet that was precisely what they *had* seen. 'He who has seen me has seen the Father' (Jn. 14:9). Traditional theology and even basic logic give way before this amazing *fact*. They have seen the invisible.

Rather more calmly and reasonably, the writer of Hebrews spells it out: God used to speak to men by His word in the mouths of the prophets, 'but in these last days he has spoken to us by a Son, whom he appointed the heir of all things, through whom also he created the world. He reflects the glory of God and bears the very stamp of his nature . . .' (Heb. 1:2, 3). He does not use the term 'image', but the idea is there. Paul makes it explicit. 'He is the image of the invisible God' (Col. 1:15), 'the likeness of God' (2 Cor. 4:4; the Greek word is the same).

We have seen that in the Old Testament the term 'image of God' was applied to man to contrast him with the rest of the animal creation, but it did not warrant us in seeing man as a special means of the revelation of God. In the New Testament this usage is still present (1 Cor. 11:7; Jas. 3:9), but alongside it comes the new idea of Christ as the image of God in a different and higher sense. Applied to Christ, the term means what in the Old Testament it could not mean, the means of God's self-revelation, the one at whom you can look and see what God is like. One can look at Jesus, as one could not look at mankind in general, and say, 'God is like that.' He who has seen Jesus has seen the Father.

The knowledge of God, then, is inextricably tied up with the knowledge of Jesus. 'This is eternal life, that they know thee the only true God, and Jesus Christ whom thou hast sent' (Jn. 17:3). Jesus cannot be by-passed: 'No one comes to the Father, but by me' (Jn. 14:6); 'no one knows the Father except the Son and any one to whom the Son chooses to reveal him' (Mt. 11:27); 'through him we . . . have access . . . to the Father' (Eph. 2:18).

This is the climax. Further than this revelation cannot go. But as with the acts of God in the Old Testament, so this supreme historical manifestation of His nature cannot be of abiding value without a parallel revelation in word. If the incarnation of the word of God is not to be a revelation limited to a very few at a single time in history, it must be reported and interpreted. And, as in the Old Testament, God provided the necessary interpreters, the apostles and evangelists, to record for later generations the facts and their meaning.

God's special definitive revelation of Himself to man is

thus through the word, the word spoken and written, and the word incarnate. The two are inextricably woven together: they are interdependent. And both come down to us in the pages of the Bible. Thus it is not strictly correct to say that God's special revelation comes through Scripture and through Christ. More exactly, it may be said to come through Scripture, and particularly through Christ as we find Him in Scripture.

But even this is not the end of the story.

The Spirit of God

It is a melancholy fact, but a very obvious one, that even the revelation of God in Scripture is not enough to bring men to the knowledge of God. There are all too many people who have the Scriptures, and who have read them perhaps with some care, and who still cannot be said to know God in the biblical sense. Their minds may be acute, and their scholarship weighty, but the Bible has not brought them beyond an academic knowledge of the nature of God. They may have acquired a full, even an impeccably sound, theology, but they do not know God.

The answer to this problem is not found in the Old Testament (though its conception of 'knowledge' goes a long way towards it, as we shall see), but emerges clearly in the New Testament, in the work of the Spirit of God. Not that the Spirit of God is absent from the Old Testament – far from it. But the New Testament reveals a further part of His work.

In the Old Testament the Spirit of God is the agent in the communication of the word of God to the prophet.[3] Thus revelation is *given* by means of the Spirit. But the new dimen-

[3] See, *e.g.*, Nu. 24:2; 2 Sa. 23:2; Ne. 9:30; Ezk. 11:5; Joel 2:28, 29; Mi. 3:8.

sion in the New Testament is His work in applying this revelation, once given, to the individual believer, bringing it to life, and leading him through it to the knowledge of God.

It was for this purpose of enlightenment, particularly with regard to His own sayings, that Jesus promised that the Holy Spirit would come to His disciples after His departure. He would bring all Jesus' sayings to their memory, bear witness to Him, guide them into all truth, and 'take what is mine and declare it to you' (Jn. 14:26; 15:26; 16:13, 14). It would be His function also to bring conviction to the unbelieving world which rejected Jesus (Jn. 16:8-11). They had the data of revelation, but without the Spirit the conviction was lacking.

Paul takes this further in that *locus classicus* on the work of the Spirit in the believer, Romans 8. His emphasis is on the contrast between two different, indeed contradictory, principles of life, those of the flesh and the Spirit. 'Those who live according to the flesh set their minds on the things of the flesh, but those who live according to the Spirit set their minds on the things of the Spirit' (verse 5). These two contrasting thought-worlds determine a man's relationship with God, whether of hostility and rebellion, leading to death (verses 6-8), or of obedience and sonship, leading to life (verses 9-17). It is the Spirit who makes this relationship of sonship a joyful reality to the believer (verses 14-16). When human weakness and ignorance would make true communion with God in prayer impossible, the Spirit comes to the believer's rescue and speaks for him (verses 26, 27).

There is thus a radical dichotomy here. Man left to himself will not, indeed cannot, respond positively to God. It takes a total reversal of his way of life and thought, which only the Spirit of God can effect, to make him capable of pleasing God and entering into a personal relationship and communication with Him. Human nature could not attain it, but the Spirit of God can lead man into it.

This line of thought comes most clearly into focus in 1 Corinthians 2, and it is worth giving some thought to this passage.

The context is the contrast and opposition between the world's idea of wisdom and the 'foolishness' of God revealed in the gospel of Christ crucified. Paul's own preaching at Corinth had been an illustration of this. He had deliberately refrained from using the language of human wisdom, and had proclaimed his 'foolish' message simply and without ostentation or bombast, relying on the power of the Spirit (verses 1-5).

Yet there is a wisdom, unknown to this world's thinkers, a 'secret and hidden wisdom of God', which Paul teaches within the ranks of believers. It is a wisdom not attained by human speculation, but revealed by the Spirit to those who love God. It is thus esoteric, given by the Spirit or not at all (verses 6-10a).

The reason for this is explained in verses 10b-16. 'The depths of God' are unattainable to man, but the Spirit of God, and He alone, searches them; only He 'comprehends the thoughts of God'. But the Spirit has been imparted to Christian believers 'that we might understand the gifts bestowed on us by God'. Thus Paul is able to teach these deep things, 'in words not taught by human wisdom, but taught by the Spirit'. Such teaching is only for 'the spiritual'. But 'the unspiritual (literally "natural") man does not receive the gifts of the Spirit of God, for they are folly to him, and he is not able to understand them because they are spiritually discerned' (verse 14). And so the amazing conclusion is reached that 'we (the "spiritual") have the mind of Christ'.

Thus knowledge of God, indeed all understanding of spiritual matters, is completely esoteric. It is not attainable by man alone, but only as he is enlightened by the Spirit, as a Christian believer. There is no true knowledge of God for the unconverted.

What then becomes of the unique status of God's special revelation through His word? Can a man not read the written word, and look at the word incarnate, and so come to know what God is like?

Yes, indeed. It is only too possible to attain a correct theology without the aid of the Spirit. The devils have it (Jas. 2:19)! But this is not to *know* God, as the Bible understands the term. For this both word and Spirit must play their part. Neither supersedes the other; both are necessary.

Thus, even though God has not left man to grope towards Himself from nature alone, but has given him a full and definitive revelation in His word, this does not mean that man now has it in his power to find God at his own convenience. The initiative is still with God, for a true knowledge of God comes only through the work of the Spirit in the individual reader or hearer of the word.

We have spoken often of a 'true knowledge of God' or of 'knowing God in the biblical sense'. We have been examining the means of reaching that knowledge. It remains now to consider what that knowledge is; and as we do so the reason for its esoteric nature will become apparent.

Knowledge of God in the Old Testament

One of the Hebrew idioms which must surely have puzzled most of us as children is this: 'Adam knew his wife' (Gn. 4:1, *etc.*; the idiom occurs seventeen times). Well, of course he knew her! Most men know their wives, don't they? Then, as we grew older and more sophisticated, we noticed that when Adam knew his wife, she conceived and bore a son, and in our wisdom we recognized one of the innumerable euphemisms for the unmentionable act of sexual intercourse.

But what an odd euphemism to choose, we must have thought. Of all the verbs available, 'know' is about the most remote from the intimate physical intercourse of man and woman. And there we would have revealed once again the immense gulf which separates the Hebrew mind (and consequently its vocabulary) from our own.

'Euphemism' it may be, but inappropriate it certainly is not. To us, knowledge is an intellectual business; to them knowledge had indeed its intellectual aspect, but that was only the end-product of a process of encounter and relationship, whose effects were not only intellectual, but moral as well. Knowledge could not be divorced from personal encounter; it included personal intimacy, and its fruit was seen in life and character as much as in understanding.

'Adam knew his wife.' And if that knowledge could be a purely intellectual one, then so might the knowledge of God! This should be enough to warn us that when we read in the Bible about knowing God, we are not in the realm of theorems and propositions. This is something living, personal, intimate.

'The sons of Eli were sons of Belial: they did not know the Lord' (1 Sa. 2:12, literally). Do you imagine that Eli, the religious leader of the nation, had never taught them their catechism? They had been brought up to know about God from the cradle. But that was as far as it went, and their lives showed it: they were 'sons of Belial'. And a son of Belial, however adequate his theology, does not know God.

The knowledge of God begins and ends in personal encounter with the living God. He does not send messages from outer space, but *meets* His people in a living, and sometimes disconcerting, relationship. Moses must stand barefoot before the burning bush, hiding his face because he was afraid to look at God, before he could receive the revelation of God's name and His purpose for His people. So it was for most of the prophets: Isaiah in the temple and Ezekiel by the river Chebar trembled before the unapproachable majesty of God and received their commission in a personal encounter which left an indelible mark on their ministry. Jeremiah dared to argue the toss with his Maker, and Jonah went one better and ran away, only to find that God has more at His command than mere words. To be the instrument of God's revelation was hardly an academic exercise.

And it is hardly to be expected that a message thus delivered should be received in cold detachment. God's revelation of Himself demands a response of repentance, worship, love, and obedience. The bald, monotheistic creed of Deuteronomy 6:4 is indissolubly yoked to the resultant demand, 'You shall love the Lord your God with all your heart, and with all your soul, and with all your might' (Dt. 6:5; one of the Aramaic Targums paraphrases the last word by 'Mammon', your wealth – hardly an academic matter!). To know God, the one true God, can mean nothing less. It cannot leave a person the same. It goes deep, below the superficial level of purely intellectual acceptance or external ritual:

'I desire steadfast love and not sacrifice,
    the knowledge of God, rather than burnt offerings'
                                      (Ho. 6:6).

To achieve this sort of knowledge of God demands more than mental gymnastics or unwavering performance of the statutory rites and ceremonies. It does not come naturally. It demands a new heart, which only God can give. 'I will give them a heart to know me, that I am the Lord; and they shall be my people and I will be their God, for they shall return to me with their whole heart' (Je. 24:7; RSV omits the first 'me', for no obvious reason except euphony). The great blessing of the covenant will be that all God's people will *know* Him, but this will only be when He has written His law in their hearts, and has forgiven and forgotten their sins (Je. 31:33, 34).

These are only a very small selection of the passages which could be cited, for this is a theme that runs right through Hebrew thought about God. God is not a theorem; He is a *person*. As such, He is only known and encountered in a total relationship which involves and affects not only the mind but the life and character as well. To know His dossier is nothing; to know *Him* is everything.

Knowledge of God in the New Testament

John seems to have been confronted by a church which lacked certainty. 'I write this to you . . . that you may *know* that you have eternal life' (1 Jn. 5:13). One thing they were not certain of was whether they really knew God. John's answer is instructive: the test is in your obedience to His commands, especially in your love. 'By this we may be sure that we know him, if we keep his commandments. He who says "I know him" but disobeys his commandments is a liar. . . . He who loves is born of God and knows God. He who does not love does not know God; for God is love' (1 Jn. 2:3, 4; 4:7, 8). To know Him is to obey Him and to reflect His very nature.

The Old Testament idea of knowing God is here repeated and even heightened. Indeed, it does not take much reading of John's letter to see that he uses 'to know God' as one of many expressions to describe true Christianity, as a personal relationship with God. It is synonymous with 'to love God', 'to abide in him', 'to be in the light', 'to be born of God', 'to be of the truth', 'to be a child of God', 'to have passed out of death into life'. A list like this gives a bird's-eye view of what it means to know God, not only in the writings of John (though he makes particular use of the phrase) but in the New Testament as a whole. It is summed up in John 17:3: 'This is eternal life, that they know thee the only true God.' What could be plainer than that?

The sons of Eli have their counterpart in the Jews who opposed Jesus. 'It is my Father who glorifies me, of whom you say that he is your God. But you have not known him; I know him' (Jn. 8:54, 55). They claimed that He was their God, and so He was, intellectually. But they did not *know* Him: their response to Jesus proved it. For all their boasted allegiance to God, they were of their father the devil (verse 44).

If you think that knowing God is a matter of passing a theological examination, try reading Philippians 3. Paul the Hebrew, Paul the Pharisee, Paul the great theologian, counted it all as so much garbage, compared with *knowing* Christ. All his theological degrees gained at the University of Jerusalem under Professor Gamaliel himself were nothing but a liability, if they kept him from the knowledge of Christ. That knowledge did not belong to the examination room, but to the cross and the tomb. It meant being like Jesus, and if that involved suffering and death, it also brought life and power. 'That I may know him and the power of his resurrection, and may share his sufferings, becoming like him in his death, that if possible I may attain the resurrection from the dead' (Phil. 3:10, 11).

Knowing God is like that: it knows no half measures. It is total commitment.

Conclusion

Our quest for the knowledge of God began with the academic question of His existence. But the Bible offered us little help on that point; it was not interested. When we turned to look at the world God has made, and men and their doings in particular, the Bible grew more enthusiastic, and guided us to some understanding of the character of the Creator, limited but exciting. Then we turned to the self-disclosure of God through His word, and the trail grew warmer, culminating in His definitive revelation of His nature in Christ. But our guide would not let us stop there, for we were still thinking in intellectual terms; we had still not arrived at the knowledge of God. Then we saw the need for the work of the Spirit to open up a realm which the intellect alone could not enter, and there we discovered the true knowledge of God in a total encounter of man with God, an encounter which involves nothing less than a new creation. The knowledge of God, as the Bible understands it, is the heart of true religion.

So when we stated that there is no knowledge of God for the unconverted, we were uttering a tautology. To know God *is* eternal life; it is the sole prerogative of the redeemed. Academic theology is open to all who have the inclination to search the world and the word for data about the deity; the knowledge of God is only for those who bow before Him in unconditional surrender and devotion. The dilettante may discover much about his Creator, but only the totally committed can know God. And they know Him not as a philosophical proposition, but as a person.

To understand this is to realize why the Bible has so little time for the question of the existence of God. Have you ever succeeded in persuading a man that his wife is an illusion? Then try to persuade one who knows God that God does not exist; your task will be no easier! The Bible has more profitable things to talk about.

4 GOD ABOVE

The Bible offers us a God to be known, personally and intimately. To some this is so outrageously incredible as to be nearly blasphemous; others accept it without a murmur, as of right. To the first, God is too remote and holy for such contact with His own creatures; to the second He is so familiar as to be almost matey. Both are right, and both are wrong, as we shall see.

The trouble with any human attempt to describe God (the present book included) is that it is bound to be inadequate. It will pick on certain aspects of the nature of God and, unless great care is taken, will allow them to be seen as the whole truth. Its selection may be more or less well balanced; it will always be inadequate.

It would be possible to devote the rest of this book to piling up different aspects of the biblical portrait of God, one on top of another, but it is doubtful if even then the reader would be much enlightened. The perfection of God is too vast, and His ways too labyrinthine, for human minds to explore and map in a leisurely hour or two. We need an Ariadne's thread to guide us.

Many scholars have tried to isolate such a thread in the Old Testament. They have sifted through the various words which the Hebrew writers loved to use about God, and have come up triumphantly with one which, for them, sums it all up, and displays in a nutshell the quintessence of God, in the light of which all other ideas fall into place and make a perfect, coherent pattern. Thus one has tried the 'personality' of God, another His 'movability', and another the idea of 'the living God'.

With this last in particular, as our first chapter will have made clear, we have much sympathy. It is, of course, a central, almost *the* central, affirmation of the Old Testament about God. But of even more value as a guide to the various key words about God in the Old Testament is the following pronouncement of T. C. Vriezen:

> 'The Old Testament religion is always dominated by two spiritual ideas, which, rationally speaking, are mutually exclusive, but which merge completely in preaching . . .: on the one hand, God is God, there is fundamental distinction between the holy God and man, so that the distance between them is infinite; and on the other hand: Of His own free will, God has entered into a direct, complete relationship with man, so that there is no distance between the Holy One and man.'[1]

Or, to put it in modern jargon, God is both transcendent and immanent. The holy God has dealings with sinful man. In a word, 'grace'.

We have been accustomed to think that it is the glory of the New Testament that in Christ the gulf between God and man is bridged, and have tended to write off the Old Testament as a religion of dutiful obedience to a distant despot. But that is altogether too superficial. Christ did indeed bridge a gulf which man could do nothing about. But grace is not the prerogative of the New Testament. It is the wonder of the Old Testament from Moses to Malachi that the holy, pure, righteous, sovereign God has deigned to have dealings at all, yes, even dealings of love, with way-

[1] *An Outline of Old Testament Theology* (ET, Blackwell), p. 147.

ward and unrewarding man. The New Testament is only the working out in full measure of the grace that is woven into the very warp and woof of the Old Testament, as it reveals to the incredulous Hebrews 'the Holy One in your midst' (Ho. 11:9).

'For thus says the high and lofty One
   who inhabits eternity, whose name is Holy:
"I dwell in the high and holy place,
   and also with him who is of a contrite and humble
    spirit" ' (Is. 57:15).

Let this, then, be our Ariadne's thread, the twin ideas of the transcendence and immanence of God, or rather the unique, incredible holding together of these two opposites in perfect harmony, which is grace. Let this be our guide to draw us back when we turn aside to the right or to the left, when we are tempted so to stress the awe-ful majesty of God that the knowledge of God seems a blasphemy, or when we are tempted to be familiar with the Almighty. Our danger is not in running to extremes – we cannot outrun the extent of either the holiness or the love of God – but in running to one extreme and forgetting the other. The correct balance in biblical theology is seldom the golden mean, the innocuous compromise, but the taking into our system of two concepts so dynamic and so opposite that they must seem to threaten to tear apart the hand that holds them.

In this chapter we shall be concerned with 'God above', with the first of our two extremes; in the next it will be the second, 'God with us'. As each is studied, never let the other be forgotten. We shall find that, though they are just about separable in theory, the Old Testament does not make it easy for us to separate them in practice. And it is with the Old Testament that these two chapters are concerned.

The holiness of God

'Transcendent' is not, of course, a biblical word. Perhaps the nearest equivalent is 'holy', and it is one of the most significant words the Old Testament applies to God. Indeed, it is God's special word, so much so that the bare adjective standing on its own can have only one meaning:

> 'To whom then will you compare me,
> that I should be like him? says *the Holy*' (Is. 40:25).

It so sums up the nature of God, that it may be used as a name for Him, and no-one could misunderstand it.

Not that nothing else is ever called 'holy'—far from it. There are holy people, holy places, holy water, holy garments, holy ointment, and holy food, to mention but a few. But they belong to God; that is what the word means. They are set apart from ordinary use, and dedicated to the use of God. Holiness is essentially not a matter of character, but of status. Ordinary things become holy not by some magical transformation, but by being dedicated to God (see, *e.g.*, Lv. 27:28). When God is in a place, it becomes 'holy ground' (Ex. 3:5), and His sanctuary is the 'holy of holies'. It is His own preserve, and it is a rare privilege indeed for a man to enter it. Israel, the people of God, are a 'holy people', because God has chosen them and set them apart for Himself (Ex. 19:5, 6; Lv. 20:26, *etc.*). Their behaviour seldom warranted any *moral* commendation, but they were none the less a holy people, in status, not in character.

There is indeed a derived moral demand in the term 'holy': the holy people must reflect something of the character of the one who has made them His own (see Lv. 19:2, and the whole ensuing chapter of moral and cere-monial demands, punctuated by the refrain, 'I am the

Lord'). But primarily 'holy', when applied to anyone or anything other than God, means simply that they are set apart and belong to Him. It is His mark of ownership.

But God Himself is holy. He too is separate, set apart from all that He has made. This is what we meant by saying that 'holy' is the nearest Old Testament equivalent to 'transcendent'. It indicates a great gulf between God and man, between God and His world. 'I am God and not man, the Holy One in your midst' (Ho. 11:9). He is poles apart. He is 'wholly other'.

That is why no man dare approach God lightly. He may rejoice in the knowledge of God, but he dare not, even then, forget the fear of God. For God is holy:

'Who is like thee, O Lord, among the gods?
Who is like thee, majestic in holiness,
terrible in glorious deeds, doing wonders?'

(Ex. 15:11).

Psalm 99 is a psalm of the holiness of God: it pictures Yahweh seated on His throne, exalted over all nations. It calls on the peoples to tremble and the earth to quake: 'Let them praise thy great and terrible name! . . . Worship at his footstool!' And repeated through the Psalm is the phrase which sums it all up: 'Holy is he!' (verses 3, 5, 9).

But to understand fully what is meant by the holiness of God, we must turn to Isaiah, who *saw* what holiness means. He was in the temple when he 'saw the Lord sitting upon a throne, high and lifted up' (Is. 6). It was a scene which caused even the seraphim, creatures of light and glory, to hide their faces. The foundations shook and smoke billowed through the temple, as one cried to the other,

'Holy, holy, holy is the Lord of hosts;
the whole earth is full of his glory.'

This is no *obiter dictum*, no thoughtless jingle. Repetition of a word in the Old Testament is a way of laying emphasis upon it, and a threefold repetition is rare indeed. When Ezekiel wanted to convey to his hearers the utter devastation which was coming to Jerusalem, he cried out, 'A ruin, ruin, ruin I will make it' (Ezk. 21:27; *cf.* also Je. 7:4). Hardly an elegant phrase, but certainly not to be taken lightly. And the 'Holy, holy, holy' of the seraphim is as emphatic an affirmation as the Hebrew language is capable of. Here is holiness to the *n*th degree.

And it took the breath out of Isaiah. 'Woe is me! For I am lost; for I am a man of unclean lips, and I dwell in the midst of a people of unclean lips; for my eyes have seen the King, the Lord of hosts!' This was no place for him; he was out of his element. The holiness of God is no environment for man to be in.

But it was not sheer terror at the burning majesty of the Wholly Other. What worried Isaiah was his uncleanness, and it was that uncleanness which the seraph purged away to enable him to stand before God. If holiness is not primarily a moral quality, this aspect cannot be removed from it, and it was in the moral purity of God that Isaiah found the greatest cause for fear.

This vision had a lasting effect on Isaiah. Not only was it the occasion when he received his commission, but it moulded his understanding of the God he was to serve. For him from now on God was supremely 'the Holy One of Israel'. It is Isaiah's special name for God, which occurs twenty-nine times in his book, and only seven times in the rest of the Old Testament. He became the prophet of holiness.

But even here, in the very heart of the transcendence of God, our Ariadne's thread cannot be forgotten, for the Holy One is the 'Holy One *of Israel*'. If Isaiah is the prophet of holiness, he is also the prophet of grace. His whole message is dominated by the amazing fact that the holy God cares for His people Israel, cares for them so much that He is prepared to act on their behalf, sinful as they are, to save them from their oppressors, and to make them, like Himself, holy. And that is the gospel in a nutshell. That is grace.

The wrath of God

The holiness of God has certain corollaries which may be unexpected. Particularly we refer to the jealousy and the wrath of God. Hear how Joshua rebuked the thoughtless determination of the people to serve Yahweh: 'You cannot serve the Lord; for he is a holy God; he is a jealous God; he will not forgive your transgressions or your sins' (Jos. 24:19). Holiness, jealousy and punishment are rolled together into a single awful deterrent. God is not to be trifled with.

Jealousy is a word we do not like. We think of it as something like envy, but worse. But there is a right jealousy, the jealousy of the husband whose love for his wife brooks no rival, who will have nothing less than the best for her, a jealousy free of suspicion and restrictive possessiveness, the inevitable result of an exclusive love. God loves His people like that, and will brook no rival to their allegiance: 'You shall not go after other gods, of the gods of the peoples who are round about you; for the Lord your God in the midst of you is a jealous God' (Dt. 6:14, 15). For God is not to be compared with other gods – He is holy, He is separate, He knows no equal, and so He is jealous, jealous of His own glory:

> 'I am the Lord, that is my name;
> my glory I give to no other,
> nor my praise to graven images' (Is. 42:8).

Even His acts of salvation for His own people are done in jealousy:

> 'For my own sake, for my own sake, I do it,
> for how should my name be profaned?
> My glory I will not give to another' (Is. 48:11).

And 'profaned' is the opposite of 'holy'. Thus God's jealousy is the inevitable corollary of His holiness.

There is a fierceness about the holiness of God which is foreign to much of our thinking. It is seen particularly in the judgment which fell on some of those who mishandled holy things. The sudden death of Nadab and Abihu, who 'offered unholy fire before the Lord', seems to us harsh and inexplicable, but Moses explained it as follows: 'This is what the Lord has said, "I will show myself holy among those who are near me, and before all the people I will be glorified" ' (Lv. 10:1-3).

There is a destructive power in holiness, not only in the holiness of God but in those things which are set apart for His service. Thus Uzzah's thoughtless handling of the ark was quickly punished (2 Sa. 6:6, 7), and the Philistines' handling of the ark when they had captured it led not only to the fall of Dagon but to their own severe discomfort, while the men of Bethshemesh who looked into it died forthwith (1 Sa. 5, 6). The reaction of their compatriots is instructive: 'Who is able to stand before the Lord, this holy God?' (1 Sa. 6:20). Holiness in the Old Testament is certainly not something mild and gentle. It can be quite terrifying.

But these cases of the fierce punishment of infringements of ritual holiness are in fact only a very small minority among the Old Testament manifestations of the wrath of God. Primarily the wrath of God is directed not against ceremonial offences but against moral evil. This too is a corollary of holiness. We have seen that the holiness of God includes the aspect of moral purity, and results in demands for moral goodness in those who have any dealings with God. The wrath of God is the result of failure to meet those demands. It is not a vindictive malice, but the inevitable reaction of the holy God to contact with sinful man. And the Old Testament is full of it. It declares the wrath of God against the nations, but particularly against His own people of Israel, to whom He had said, 'You shall be holy to me; for I the Lord am holy, and have separated you from the peoples, that you should be mine' (Lv. 20:26). His anger and His punishment fell upon them not simply because they were imperfect, but because

'they have rejected the law of the Lord of hosts,
    and have despised the word of the Holy One of Israel'
                                                    (Is. 5:24).

There is no need for a catalogue of Old Testament references to the wrath of God. But the point to be made here is that His wrath and His jealousy are not regrettable lapses in an otherwise passable record, but the inevitable out-working of a holiness which is not simply an exclusive 'otherness' but a perfect moral purity.

The glory of God

If 'holiness' is the nearest Old Testament equivalent to 'transcendence', a close second to it would be 'glory'. The unapproachable majesty and dazzling brightness of God marks Him out as 'the King of glory' (Ps. 24:7-10).

The most usual Hebrew word for glory is derived from the verb 'to be heavy', and it can refer to literal 'abundance' of possessions, as well as to 'honour' and 'glory'. Indeed, there is often something almost tangible about the glory of God. It is objective, visible. It sometimes seems almost to be detached from God Himself, and to become a 'thing' which moves about, its coming and going signifying the presence and absence of God. And when it comes, it is greeted with awe and even fear, as well as with rejoicing in the presence of the Lord of glory.

It came to Ezekiel by the river Chebar, and he struggled valiantly to describe it. But words fail, and generation after generation has tried to work out exactly what he *did* see, and just how the mechanics of the wheels worked, and what the eyes were doing, and which creatures had which face where, and so on. But does it really matter? It was the incredible vehicle of a still greater wonder, for 'above the firmament over their heads there was the likeness of a throne, in appearance like sapphire; and seated above the likeness of a throne was a likeness as it were of a human form' (Ezk. 1:26). Could he make it any clearer that he is describing the indescribable? 'Likeness', 'appearance', 'as it were', no less than thirteen times in three verses. This is not clinical analysis, but the memory of an overwhelming and altogether indescribable encounter with the transcendent. 'Such was the appearance of the likeness of the glory of the Lord. And when I saw it, I fell upon my face' (1:28).

But if Ezekiel's description of the visible glory of God is unique in its completeness, he was certainly not the first to *see* God's glory localized in a particular place. In the wilderness 'the glory of the Lord appeared in the cloud' (Ex. 16:10), it 'settled on Mount Sinai', looking like a devouring fire (Ex. 24: 16, 17), and when the tabernacle was completed the glory of the Lord filled it (Ex. 40:34, 35). Many times in the wilderness period God assured His people of His presence, for blessing or judgment, in the visible form of His 'glory' (*e.g.* Lv. 9:23; Nu. 14:10; 16:19, 42). Solomon's temple, too, was visited at its dedication by the glory of the Lord, so that the priests could not enter (1 Ki. 8:11 = 2 Ch. 5:14; 2 Ch. 7:1-3), and the glory which Ezekiel saw was the symbol of God's departure from the old temple and return to the new one (Ezk. 10:4, 18, 19; 11:22, 23; 43:2-5). Usually it is described in terms of cloud and fire, and always there is the fear and wonder of the presence of God Himself (see especially Dt. 5:22-26).

But God's glory is seen not only in this specific visible form, but in all that He has made and in all that He has done. The heavens declare it (Ps. 19:1) and the earth is full of it (Is. 6:3). The Psalms are full of the glory and majesty of God (e.g. Pss. 8:1; 96:3, 6-8), and call all men to fall down and worship. Isaiah, the prophet of holiness, is also the prophet of the glory of God; indeed the two are inseparable. He sees it already revealed to men (Is. 6:3; cf. 42:8; 48:11), but particularly looks forward to the future restoration of God's people and the coming of the Messiah, when the glory of the Lord will be plain for all to see.[2] Then, while His enemies shrink in terror from His glory and majesty (Is. 2:10, 19, 21),

> 'The earth will be filled
> with the knowledge of the glory of the Lord,
> as the waters cover the sea'
>
> (Hab. 2:14; cf. Is. 11:9).

The glory of God, then, is something which men are to be aware of; it is meant to be 'seen'. But to see it is to realize the immense gulf which separates man from God, and to fall in awe and worship, even terror, before this majestic Lord. It is often spoken of in connection with light (Ps. 104:1, 2; Hab. 3:3, 4) or fire (Ex. 24:17; Dt. 5:24). It is dazzling, even dangerous, for mortal man. Moses was refused a direct sight, for his own good (Ex. 33:18-23). To see the glory of God is a privilege, but it is also a risk, and no man dare take it lightly. For it is an expression of His holiness, of His complete separation from all that is mortal and imperfect. It reveals His transcendence.

[2] Is. 11:10; 35:2; 40:5; 59:19; 60:1, 2, etc.

The eternity of God

'In the beginning, God . . .'. The Old Testament never doubts, and frequently affirms, in the strongest terms, the eternity of God. When the world began, He was simply 'there', and the final dissolution of the creation will make no difference to Him.

'They will perish, but thou dost endure;
 they will all wear out like a garment.
Thou changest them like raiment, and they pass away;
 but thou art the same, and thy years have no end'
(Ps. 102:26, 27).

He has no beginning and no end. He does not change or evolve. He is simply 'the everlasting God' (Gn. 21:33; Is. 40:28).

'Before the mountains were brought forth,
 or ever thou hadst formed the earth and the world,
 from everlasting to everlasting thou art God' (Ps. 90:2).

The other religions of the ancient Near East took great delight in tales of the events before the creation, which included the birth of their chief gods. They had genealogies and family histories for gods as well as men. But of all this the Old Testament shows no trace. Man is born and dies; the world itself grows old. But God is the first and the last (Is. 44:6; 48:12); He does not change (Mal. 3:6). He lives for ever (Dn. 12:7). In fact He stands completely outside time:

'A thousand years in thy sight
 are but as yesterday when it is past,
 or as a watch in the night' (Ps. 90:4).

Such a God is one who can safely be relied on for protection and deliverance.

'Trust in the Lord for ever,
    for the Lord God
    is an everlasting rock'
                (Is. 26:4; *cf.* Dt. 33:27).

The majestic description of God the incomparable Creator in Isaiah 40 is designed to make just this point. They thought He did not care, or even did not know of their plight (verse 27).

'Have you not known? Have you not heard?
The Lord is the everlasting God,
    the Creator of the ends of the earth.
He does not faint or grow weary,
    his understanding is unsearchable' (verse 28).

You can rely on a God like that.

But it is the Psalms that particularly rejoice in God's eternity, and always the emphasis falls on the contrast between the nations who set themselves against God, whose plans are doomed to frustration, and the eternal God, whose counsel 'stands for ever, the thoughts of his heart to all generations' (Ps. 33:11). He sits enthroned as King and Judge over all who dispute His authority, and there can be no rival to His dominion, for it is without beginning and without end.

'Thy throne is established from of old;
    thou art from everlasting' (Ps. 93:2).

'Thy kingdom is an everlasting kingdom,
    and thy dominion endures throughout all generations'
                (Ps. 145:13).[3]

---

[3] *Cf.* also Pss. 9:7; 10:16; 29:10; 92:8; 102:12.

And in the eternal reign of God His people's security is assured. This conviction has made the saints of all ages invincible. They have faced the scorn and oppression of the rulers of this world, and seen them to be petty and ephemeral. They have faced the lions, the stake, and the labour camp, and known that the last word had not yet been spoken. Their doctrine of the eternity of God has been expressed not so much in a learned treatise as in a shout of victory:

> 'The Lord will reign for ever,
>   thy God, O Zion, to all generations.
> Praise the Lord!' (Ps. 146:10).

The almighty Creator

One of the traditional 'attributes of God' in any standard doctrinal treatment must be His omnipotence. Now there are in fact a few almost formal statements of the omnipotence of God in the Old Testament.[4] God is known, moreover, as *El Shaddai*, which our English versions have translated as 'God Almighty'. But it is by no means certain that this is the meaning of the name, and in the book of Job in particular '*Shaddai*' has clearly become just a title for God, used without special reference to its original meaning, whatever that was. It is certainly a title of majesty and sovereignty, but it cannot be claimed as an explicit ascription of omnipotence to God. So the search for systematic formulations of the divine omnipotence in the Old Testament is likely to be a frustrating one.

But by now this ought not to surprise us. The Old Testament is not given to systematic formulations, and bears disturbingly little resemblance to a textbook of doctrine. It presents a Person.

[4] Jb. 42:2; Ps. 115:3; Dn. 4:35; Je. 32:27; and *cf.* Gn. 18:14a.

And so the omnipotence of God is seen in action, not in theory. It is seen in the history of His people, in His miraculous protection, His might in war and His judgment on the nations. But above all it is seen in His creation.

Creation is the sole prerogative of God. 'To create' is His own special verb, and it never has any other subject in the Old Testament. It is one of those words whose very appearance alerts the reader that something big is coming. Other verbs are, of course, used: to 'make', to 'form', to 'establish' and so on. But these are all things that men can do. Only God can 'create'. It implies a new beginning, and the idea of supernatural power is never far from it. If it does not explicitly teach that God created the world out of nothing, it is hard to see how anything else could satisfy so portentous a verb.

The word occurs, of course, in the early chapters of Genesis, and sporadically throughout the Old Testament, but it is in the later chapters of Isaiah that it really comes into its own: chapters 40-66 contain nearly half of its total uses. To a people in exile, whose trust in God had failed, and with it all hope for the future, the prophet presents God the Creator. In chapter after chapter he reminds them that God created all that is, and such a God brooks no rivals.

'Thus says the Lord
who created the heavens
    (he is God!),
who formed the earth and made it
    (he established it;
he did not create it a chaos,
    he formed it to be inhabited!):
"I am the Lord, and there is no other" ' (Is. 45:18).

(It would be worth learning Hebrew even to read this verse alone! Isaiah 40:12-26 expands the same idea.)

His purpose cannot be thwarted, for all that passes in His world, light and darkness, weal and woe, comes from His creative will (45:5-7). His wisdom and His power are unquestionable (45:9-13), and there is no limit to His care for those He has created (43:1-7; *cf.* 40:25-31). His creation is no mere piece of ancient history, but constantly He watches over His creation in sovereign power, and still He creates new things, new situations, new purposes. The Persian conquest of Babylon, which was to release the Jews from their exile, was to be His creative work (45:8; this is the point of all the stress on creation in chapter 45), and still further ahead the creative will and power of God will not be dimmed:

'For behold, I create new heavens and a new earth;
and the former things shall not be remembered
or come into mind' (Is. 65:17).

No brief summary can do justice to the grandeur of these superb chapters. Read them and see, and you will know more of the real meaning of God's creation (and His omnipotence) than you would learn from a hundred books of doctrinal analysis. You will see the wisdom, and the power, and the love of God for His people, and you will not dare to doubt Him again.

Space forbids any further study of the Old Testament's view of God as the Creator. We looked at it from another angle in chapter 2,[5] and inevitably it creeps in at many other points. It is fundamental to the Hebrew idea of God, and with it it carries His almighty power, and His unsearchable wisdom. It is one of the richest veins in all this fabulous mine of spiritual treasure.

[5] See above, pp. 29-33.

The sovereignty of God

If the heavens and the earth owe their origin to the creative act of God, then it follows that

'The earth is the Lord's and the fullness thereof,
   the world and those who dwell therein' (Ps. 24:1).

We have seen already how the Psalms delight to declare that God's throne is established, and He will reign for ever. Psalms 93, 97 and 99 begin with the triumphant cry, 'The Lord is King!', and many more echo the same idea. And He is King not only over Israel but over all the nations. There is nothing parochial about the Psalms: one after another declares the universal lordship of God over all nations, whether for blessing or for judgment (see, *e.g.*, Pss. 2, 47, 67, 96). He did not make the world and its inhabitants and then leave them to run riot. All that He has made is under His firm control, man no less than nature, and pagan no less than Israel.

This sovereignty of God over His creation has many aspects, some of which will come to light in the next chapter. But one of the most striking is the unshakable conviction of Israel that God ruled the thoughts and actions even of those who deliberately opposed Him, or even knew nothing of Him. Proverbs points this out with reference to the individual:

'A man's mind plans his way,
   but the Lord directs his steps' (Pr. 16:9; *cf.* 16:1).
'Many are the plans in the mind of a man,

   but it is the purpose of the Lord that will be established'
                              (Pr. 19:21; *cf.* 20:24).

But it is most clearly seen writ large in the history of the

74

nations. As one world empire after another sent its armies storming irresistibly across the barren deserts of the Middle East, the Old Testament prophets saw behind each the hand of the One

'who brings princes to nought,
   and makes the rulers of the earth as nothing' (Is. 40:23).

As the cruel and godless Assyrian army marched on northern Israel, God hailed them through Isaiah,

'Ah, Assyria, the rod of *my* anger,
   the staff of *my* fury!
Against a godless nation *I* send him,
   and against the people of my wrath *I* command him'
                                            (Is. 10: 5, 6).

What superb assurance! But was it justified? Read on, and you will find that Assyria knew nothing of this mission, but was engaged in its usual mission of empire-building carnage, for its own aggrandisement, and confident in its own unassailable strength. But the prophet is not daunted by human boasting, even from the acknowledged masters of the earth.

'Shall the axe vaunt itself over him who hews with it,
   or the saw magnify itself against him who wields it?'
                                            (10:15).

So, when the Lord has finished His mission of judgment on Israel, the arrogance of Assyria too will meet its punishment (10:12, 16-19).

Then came Babylon, and Jeremiah was not afraid to draw the same conclusion: 'Thus says the Lord of hosts: Because you have not obeyed my words, behold, I will send for all the tribes of the north, says the Lord, and for Nebuchadrezzar the king of Babylon, *my servant*, and I will bring them against this land . . .' (Je. 25:8, 9). Nebuchadrezzar had, as yet, no more knowledge of God than the Assyrians, and Babylon, if more refined, was far from blameless; it too must suffer in its turn (25:12-14). But for the moment Nebuchadrezzar, whether he liked it or not, was God's servant.

This is no easy teaching to accept. It takes a very big and a very trusting conception of God to see His hand behind the destruction of your own nation, especially when perpetrated by a godless and wicked nation. We would not find it easy to claim Mao Tse-tung as God's servant. For Habakkuk at least it was too much.

His problem was that God seemed to let wickedness go on unchecked around him (Hab. 1:2-4). But God's answer made matters worse (1:5-11). It was out of the frying-pan into the fire. For God's solution was to send the Chaldeans (the Babylonians) against His own people. And He was not at all unaware of their character; indeed He made it only too clear to Habakkuk. The prophet takes the point that this is God's method of punishing His people (1:12), but he will not take it lying down; he protests (1:13-17).

> 'Thou who art of purer eyes than to behold evil
>   and canst not look on wrong,
> why dost thou look on faithless men,
>   and art silent when the wicked swallows up
>   the man more righteous than he?'

He never receives a full answer; perhaps no man ever has. But he takes his stand on the watch-tower to wait for the Lord's response, and when it comes, it satisfies him. It is that 'he whose soul is not upright in him shall fail' (2:4), and the 'woes' of the rest of the chapter spell out in some detail the fate that awaits the Chaldeans in their turn; wickedness is not to go unpunished. For behind their exultant progress stands the Lord, who sent them to fulfil His purpose.

'The Lord is in his holy temple;
  let all the earth keep silence before him' (2:20).

It is His purpose which will finally be established, and His glory which will fill the earth (2:14). It is for the man of God to take his stand on this assurance of the sovereignty of the holy God, and to know that the sufferings of the present are not the final word. It is not by questioning the wisdom of God, but by trust in His sovereignty and His justice, that the righteous shall live (2:4).

And so Babylon conquered, and the Jews set out for their long exile. To them it seemed the end, but not to God, whose purpose is not limited to a human generation or two. And so, in the fullness of time, 'that the word of the Lord by the mouth of Jeremiah might be accomplished, the Lord stirred up the spirit of Cyrus king of Persia . . .' (Ezr. 1:1) and the Jews were set free to return to their own land. We have not the space to study in detail here Isaiah's magnificent prophetic commentary on God's choice and direction of Cyrus for the overthrow of Babylon (Is. 44:21-45:13), but again the same pattern emerges of a world conqueror with no knowledge of God (45:4, 5) directed in his triumphant campaign to the fulfilment of the purpose of the sovereign God, Creator and Controller of the world and all that is in it.

Today men cringe from such an unqualified ascription to God of the course of world history. We are willing to credit Him with our victories, but not with our defeats, with the achievements of man at his best but not with the atrocities of man at his worst. But there is little today to match the vicious cruelty of Assyria, and yet it was in this that Isaiah saw the hand of God. It is not that the quality of history has altered, but that there are few today whose conception of God matches that of Isaiah. Its audacity is breath-taking, its faith superb. His reckoning begins not with the puzzles of life on earth, but with the certainty of a Creator God. From this vantage-point he sees our human predicament in perspective, and above our mealy-mouthed apologies for a God whose sovereignty and whose wisdom we only half credit, his strident voice cries out, 'Your God is too small!'

Part of the trouble, for Israel as for us, is that we regard God as our exclusive possession, and His favour and protection as our right. You have only to remember as far back as the last War to see that. It was Amos in particular whose job it was to prick this bubble. His book opens with fierce denunciations of the wickedness of the surrounding nations, and prophecies of their doom, and no doubt his audience clapped and cheered. But the applause must have died away very quickly as chapter 2 followed on, with the same denunciations and worse for Judah and Israel. Yet they *were* God's chosen people—and *therefore* their punishment was the more certain (Am. 3:2).

> ' "Are you not like the Ethiopians to me,
>   O people of Israel?" says the Lord.
> "Did I not bring up Israel from the land of Egypt . . .?" '
> (Am. 9:7).

Oh yes, they knew that all right, and gloried in this token of God's exclusive favour to them—

> ' ". . . and the Philistines from Caphtor
>   and the Syrians from Kir?" '

He is no petty tribal God. His concern, and His control, are world-wide. His sovereignty is absolute.

> 'It is he who sits above the circle of the earth,
>   and its inhabitants are like grasshoppers;
> who stretches out the heavens like a curtain,
>   and spreads them like a tent to dwell in;
> who brings princes to nought,

and makes the rulers of the earth as nothing'

(Is. 40:22, 23).

And you would have to go a long way to find a better paraphrase of 'transcendent' than that!

This, then, is the God of the Old Testament, the God of Abraham, and Moses, and David, and Isaiah, *and*, though they did not know it, the God of Sargon, and Nebuchadrezzar, and Cyrus, and Alexander. A God to be feared; a God to be worshipped; a God to be reckoned with; a God who breaks out of the strait jacket of man's loftiest thought and noblest theology, with a glory and a majesty that dazzles and bewilders the holiest saint. God transcendent. God above.

5 GOD WITH US

The English army was hopelessly outnumbered at Agincourt. But as they waited miserably for the unequal battle, the king himself went round among them, nobles and common soldiers alike, cheering, encouraging with an infectious confidence, with the result

'That every wretch, pining and pale before,
Beholding him, plucks comfort from his looks'.

The battle of Agincourt was won not so much by arms or strategy, as by

'A little touch of Harry in the night'.

A similar though far higher wonder thrills and amazes the biblical writers as they survey the dealings of God with His world. He is transcendent, the holy One, dwelling in unapproachable glory. But He has not kept His distance, and commanded His world by remote control; still less has He left it to its own devices. He is involved, deeply and intimately, in all the affairs of the world at large and of every man, woman and child in it. The God above is also 'God with us'.

So inescapable is this fact that already, in outlining the transcendence of God, we have inevitably touched again and again on His involvement in His world. The idea of God as Creator particularly holds the two truths together, the 'wholly other' existence of the God who was there before the worlds were made and who will outlast them all, whose word of power brought them into being, and His concern and care for the world He has made, His continued direction of its course and of everything and everyone in it. We have seen in particular His sovereignty over men, emphasising at one and the same time His unquestionable pre-eminence over any created power and His uncompromising involvement in even the most sordid and trivial of their doings. We have spoken too in a previous chapter of the amazing truth that a man can know God, not simply by studying Him afar off, but in an intimate personal relationship with the transcendent Lord. It remains in this chapter to trace further the incredible involvement of 'the high and lofty One, who inhabits eternity, whose name is Holy' in the affairs of His humble creation.

The providence of God

We have already had cause to refer several times to God the Creator of the world and all that is in it. It may have been noticed, however, particularly when we looked for a revelation of God in nature,[1] that the passages studied spoke more of what God *is* doing constantly in the world, than of the original act of creation. Even that portentous verb, to 'create',[2] applies not only to the original creation in Genesis 1, but to what God is doing, and *will* do, in the world.

Modern Western man sees the world as running in conformity with fixed 'laws of nature'. He may or may not ascribe the origin of those laws to God, but he sees little place for God in the implementation of them. Once estab-

[1] Above, pp. 29-33.
[2] Above, pp. 72-73.

lished, they work themselves out inexorably, and God is entitled to a well-earned rest as He sits back and watches His well-oiled machinery run itself. Automation has taken over even in heaven.

We would not call ourselves deists, even those of us who know what the word means, but we are perilously close to those free-thinkers of the seventeenth and eighteenth centuries who saw no role for God in His world after the initial act of creation.

But, you may object, surely we still believe that God can and does intervene in the affairs of the world. And in so saying, you reveal the gulf which separates our modern thinking from that of the Bible. We talk of miracles as God breaking into or reversing the natural order, which is assumed to be independent of God. But for the Hebrew mind, the 'natural order' was itself the constant work of God. If He chooses to act in an unexpected or unusual way, this should be no cause for surprise. Is He not free to run His world as He wishes? But talk of 'intervention' would be meaningless to them: all the world's course, the usual as well as the unusual, is the direct work of God. Nothing happens automatically – God does it.

It is no accident that many of the passages which outline the creative activity of God are expressed in a series of active participles. 'The participle active indicates a person or thing conceived as being in the continual uninterrupted exercise of an activity.'[3] Nor is it by accident that our English versions have often ignored this fact, and translated the participle by a simple past tense, 'created', 'stretched out', *etc.* The RSV is a prime offender in this respect.[4] Is this another indication of the latent deism of modern Western thinking, which prefers to speak of once-for-all creation in

[3] Gesenius-Kautzsch, *Hebrew Grammar* (ET, Oxford University Press), section 116a.
[4] See, *e.g.*, Jb. 9:8, 9; Ps. 104:2, 3; Is. 42:5; 44:24; 45:18.

the past rather than of the continuous creative activity of God?

At least for the Old Testament there is no doubt that every movement of the stars and the seasons (Jb. 38:31-33; Is. 40:26; Am. 5:8), every change of the weather (Jb. 38), every part of the life-cycle of the meanest creature on earth (Jb. 39ff.; Ps. 104) is the direct work of God the Creator. In practice the round of the seasons is predictable, but this is only because God has decided to make it so (Gn. 8:22); if there is a fixed order, it is because God has made a covenant to keep it so (Je. 31:35, 36; 33:20, 25).

Given such a conception of the relation between God and His world, it is hardly surprising that miracles occasion little difficulty for the Old Testament writers. For 'miracles' are simply the times when God decides to work in a different way from the normal. They are no more and no less the work of God than is the ordinary course of events. God is at liberty to run His creation as He wishes.

The affairs of men stem from the same continuous creative activity of God. Their birth (Gn. 4:1, 25; 18:10), their breath (Gn. 2:7; Ps. 104:30; Is. 42:5), their food (Pss. 104:27, 28; 145:15, 16), their going out and coming in (Ps. 121:8), and their death (Ps. 104:29) are all determined by Him. He teaches them their skills, farming (Is. 28:24-29, especially verses 26, 29), metal-working (Is. 54:16), and other craftsmanship (Ex. 31:2-5), and even fighting (Ps. 144:1). We have seen above[5] that all a man's actions, whatever his intentions may be, are directed by God. They may give themselves credit for their achievements, as did Sennacherib of Assyria for his triumphant march across the Levant, but God thought otherwise:

> 'Have you not heard
> that I determined it long ago?

[5] See pp. 74 ff.

I planned from days of old
        what now I bring to pass'
                        (2 Ki. 19:25=Is. 37:26).

And, as usual, God had the last word.

One of the fullest and most remarkable expressions of this concern of God with every one of His creatures in all their thoughts and deeds is Psalm 139. God knows all that a man does, every thought of his mind before it even turns into words (verses 1-6). It is impossible to escape from His scrutiny, or from His protecting and guiding hand, for all the corners of the earth, and heaven, and even the abode of the dead, are open to Him; indeed already He is 'there' (verses 7-12; *cf.* verse 18). God it is who creates every man in the first place, who performs the ever new miracle of conception and birth (verses 13-15), and His concern does not finish with the launching of a human life, but covers every phase of it, for

'In thy book were written, every one of them,
the days that were formed for me,
        when as yet there was none of them' (verse 16).

The psalmist concludes that, since God's scrutiny is inevitable, the right way is to submit freely to that scrutiny and to God's direction of his life, 'in the way everlasting' (verses 23, 24).

And what is true of the life of the individual is true also of human history on the larger scale. It is not just that God watches and permits: He directs. Empires rise and fall, but it is the Lord who does it (Is. 40:23, 24). The amazing success of Cyrus suggests a power behind the throne. Who can it be?

'I, the Lord, the first,
        and with the last; I am He' (Is. 41:2-4).

Even where it is hard to see the hand of God, the faith of the prophets traced its operation.[6]

> 'Does evil befall a city,
>   unless the Lord has done it?' (Am. 3:6).

By and large, the Old Testament writers do not trouble to defend the rightness of the way God directs history. For them it is enough that it *is* God who directs it, and the faith of Abraham upholds their confidence in the face of the puzzles of providence: 'Shall not the Judge of all the earth do right?' (Gn. 18:25). But in spite of this plea of Abraham, Sodom was destroyed, for not even ten righteous men were in it (Gn. 18:32; 19:24, 25). God is not squeamish, and judgment is a reality, as well on Israel as on other nations. The Amalekites were not to be wiped out from sheer wanton cruelty and bloodlust, but as a punishment (1 Sa. 15:2, 3). For the men of the Old Testament, that was enough. If this was God's judgment, they were prepared to accept it.

But the sterner aspect of God's dealings with His world and the men who inhabit it is not the whole story.

The love of God

It can never have been easy to be a prophet. They found themselves in many unenviable situations, with an unpopular message to deliver, often suffering physically for their faithfulness, and sometimes called upon to perform symbolic actions which were at best embarrassing, and often absurd and very uncomfortable. But surely the hardest lot fell to Hosea, for his prophetic calling involved him in nothing less than a broken marriage. Yet as he lavished his love on a worthless woman, and felt the bitterness of her

[6] See above, pp. 75-78.

desertion and adultery, and as his love still pursued her and took her back after it all, the whole episode was the most potent symbol of the love of God, free and undeserved, yet spurned and suffering, and still pursuing His truant people with a faithfulness that knows no defeat, to restore them at last to the privileges of the covenant which they themselves had broken.

Hosea's is the most dramatic of many Old Testament attempts to explore the love of God, especially the love of God for His people Israel. Many of them use the metaphor of marriage, and it is a telling one. But all metaphors have their limitations.

Love is blind, they say, and yet human love, especially when it has an eye to marriage, has a canny way of overcoming this disability. It may be blind to many problems, but it usually has good reasons for its choice. In other words, we love because we find something lovable in the other. We love them for what they are. And that is where the metaphor breaks down.

Why did God choose to love Israel, of all peoples? Certainly not because there was any sort of equality:

> 'Behold, to the Lord your God belong heaven and the heaven of heavens, the earth with all that is in it; yet the Lord set his heart in love upon your fathers and chose their descendants after them, you above all peoples, as at this day' (Dt. 10:14, 15).

Were they then particularly attractive morally?

> 'Know therefore, that the Lord your God is not giving you this good land to possess because of your righteousness; for you are a stubborn people' (Dt. 9:6).

Perhaps, then, there was a political motive: was Israel a strategic prize?

'It was not because you were more in number than
any other people that the Lord set his love upon you
and chose you, for you were the fewest of all peoples'
(Dt. 7:7),

and this same passage goes on to bring out the true reason
for this remarkable choice by the Lord of heaven and earth –
'but it is because the Lord loves you'. There it is, as
gloriously illogical as any romantic novel could dream up:
God has set His love upon them because He loves them!
And yet how profoundly satisfying. There *could* be no other
reason for so unequal a match, and if there were, the
marriage would soon be on the rocks. It is sheer undeserved,
unconditioned, free love.

The extended metaphor of Ezekiel 16 makes this point
with a forcefulness which is too much for modern sensitivity,
with its vivid description of the untended outcast child
whom Yahweh took up to be the object of His love. That is
how God loves, and it is well for man that He does, or he
would know nothing of the love of God.

We have inevitably, in speaking of the love of God for
Israel, introduced the idea of 'choice'; inevitably, because
this is the way the Old Testament sees it. The love of God
is a love which chooses, and the verbs 'love' and 'choose' are
often combined in describing the origin of that special
relationship which Israel enjoyed with God (*e.g.* Dt. 4:37;
7:6, 7; 10:15); indeed, in this context there is little to
choose between the meanings of the two verbs.[7] They refer
particularly to the crucial event of the deliverance from
Egypt, as the time when God's choice of Israel to be His
people was effectively implemented.

'When Israel was a child, I loved him,
and out of Egypt I called my son' (Ho. 11:1).

[7] See especially Mal. 1:2, 3; Gn. 29:30, 31 for the use of 'love' and
'hate' in the sense of 'choose' and 'reject'.

And this choice, this love for Israel, is exclusive:

'You only have I known
   of all the families of the earth' (Am. 3:2).

But in this too it is like human love, especially the love which culminates in marriage. Such love makes a choice, for better or worse, a choice which binds two people in an exclusive relationship for life. To love someone else in the same way is to be guilty of breaking the relationship – it is adultery. Such is the love of God for Israel, free and undeserved, but exclusive, even jealous, as all true love must be. For better or worse, Yahweh has selected His bride.

The faithfulness of God

But there is more to marriage than loving and choosing a partner. That is only the first step. Marriage itself is a contract, a covenant, between the two parties, and the thing that makes a marriage work is the faithfulness of those two parties in observing the contract, for better or worse. That is the real test of love.

So God has entered into a covenant with Israel, His chosen. This idea of the covenant is at the centre of Old Testament thinking about the relationship of God with man. It is the foundation on which all the religion of Israel rests. We cannot study it in detail here. Suffice it to say that a covenant involves obligations on both parties, faithfulness to which keeps it intact. If the obligations are not met, the covenant is broken.

The obligations attaching to God's covenant with His people are summed up in the phrase, 'You shall be my people, and I will be your God' (Ex. 6:7; Lv. 26:12; Je. 7:23; 11:4, *etc.*). Israel's obligations are spelled out in more detail in the Ten Commandments, and more fully still in all the stipulations of the law given at Sinai, when the covenant was made in its definitive form. But all these laws are simply expositions of what it means to be God's people. 'Now therefore, if you will obey my voice and keep my covenant, you shall be my own possession among all peoples' (Ex. 19:5).

But God too has entered into a commitment that He will be their God, that He will stand by them, dwell among them, lead them and watch over them with His special favour. Not that He was under any compulsion to do so. This is no bilateral agreement hammered out between equals, but an agreement imposed 'from above', because God would have it so. But He has chosen to commit Himself. Here more than anywhere else we see the incredible condescension of the Lord of heaven and earth, that He has chosen to bind Himself to an insignificant nation of fugitives, whose stubbornness and perversity He knew well enough. But He has so chosen, and having given His word, He will not go back on it. The covenant stands, the marriage is solemnized, and Yahweh is bound to be Israel's God, for better or worse.

And it is in this context that we are introduced to one of the most wonderful, and certainly one of the most untranslatable, words in the Old Testament, *chesed*. The AV generally renders it 'mercy', sometimes 'loving-kindness', 'goodness', *etc*. The RSV is more accurate and consistent in its use of 'steadfast love', or sometimes 'faithfulness'. Others have suggested 'loyal love', 'loving fidelity' and many others. It is a blend of love and faithfulness, with a touch of compassion. But above all it is a word of the covenant. 'To keep covenant and *chesed*' is a common phrase, and in Isaiah 55:3 'covenant' and *chesed* are used as synonyms.

There are other words for God's dealings with men, 'mercy', 'grace', 'compassion', and the like. They are words which speak of the kindness of a superior to an inferior, who has no claim at all on that kindness. They are wonderful words, words on which man's whole salvation depends. But there is something still more wonderful about *chesed*. All men may enjoy 'grace' and 'mercy', but only God's chosen people are the objects of *chesed*. It is His special care for those to whom He has bound Himself in covenant. If unmerited favour is wonderful, still more wonderful is that divine condescension which is willing to be bound to an undeserving race, to place Himself freely under an obligation to love and to cherish His people to the end.

It is love (*ahabah*) that launches a marriage, but it is *chesed* that makes a go of it, and God does nothing by halves. So His *ahabah* inevitably involves *chesed*:

> 'I have loved you with an everlasting love (*ahabah*);
> therefore I have continued my *chesed* to you' (Je. 31:3).

And it is well for Israel that it is so. For their part, they could never get within sight of fulfilling their covenant obligations. As the people of God they were always an embarrassment, and often a complete disgrace, and they even revelled in their unfaithfulness. But God is not like that; His nature is one of *chesed*. He cannot abandon the people He has chosen. He will have no divorce. The whole Old Testament is the story of Israel's constant faithlessness, and of God's love constantly reaching out to draw them back to their covenant with Him. It is the story of *chesed*, and there is nothing quite so moving.

> 'Wonderful as is His love for His covenant people, His steady persistence in it is more wonderful still. The most important of all the distinctive ideas of the Old Testament is God's steady and extraordinary persis-

tence in continuing to love wayward Israel in spite of Israel's insistent waywardness.'[8]

That is *chesed*.

If Hosea was the prophet of *ahabah*, he was still more the prophet of *chesed*.[9] Here was a marriage hopelessly broken, a clear case for the divorce court. But Hosea did not want a divorce; he wanted his bride back again, and he searched for her, and bought her back from the slave-market, to be his own once more. Such is the love of God. Israel had deserted Him, and Hosea emphasized this by giving his children the names 'Not pitied' and 'Not my people', 'for you are not my people and I am not your God' (1:9). But *chesed* does not so easily admit defeat; God will yet win Israel back,

'And I will have pity on Not pitied,
and I will say to Not my people, "You are my people";
and he shall say, "Thou art my God" ' (2:23).

The covenant will be restored. God cannot let it lapse.

Sometimes Israel went too far, and punishment was inevitable. But this did not mean an end to God's *chesed*, for always there was a remnant through whom the covenant was preserved. God saw to that. Unreliable as Israel proved to be, the reliability of God was greater. The word most commonly linked with *chesed* is *emeth*, 'faithfulness', 'reliability'. It comes from the same root as 'Amen', and means that which is confirmed, established, unshakable. The two words together provide eloquent testimony to the utterly dependable faithfulness of God. What He has taken in hand, He will surely complete. His loving purpose for

[8] N. H. Snaith, *The Distinctive Ideas of the Old Testament* (Epworth Press), p. 102.
[9] Surprisingly Hosea only once uses the word *chesed* with God as subject: 2:19.

Israel will triumph, even though Israel herself is the chief obstacle to it.

And so it was that the prophets came to look forward not simply to a constant renewal of a constantly broken covenant, but to a new covenant. It will not be like the old covenant, which was so regularly sabotaged (Je. 31:31, 32), but will have a surer foundation: the law of their Lord will be written no longer only on stone tablets, but on their hearts, and their relationship with Him will no longer be second-hand (Je. 31:33, 34). Hitherto the barrier to the success of the covenant had been Israel's own rebellious nature; now they will be given a new heart (Ezk. 36:25ff.). Then they will be truly His people, and He their God (Je. 31:33; Ezk. 36:28), the covenant will be finally established, and the *chesed* of God triumphant. Yahweh will rejoice in His bride, and she in Him, for ever.

The righteousness of God

Of all the uninviting words of an old-fashioned religious jargon, 'righteousness' is one of the worst. If it means anything at all to the average man, it expresses a stuffy legalism, prim and unattractive, or at best it is a Victorian synonym for good deeds. It is certainly not exciting.

The AV tried valiantly to confine the Hebrew words *tsedeq* and *tsedaqah* in the same strait jacket, by translating them always by 'justice' or 'righteousness' and their cognates, and in so doing missed the point completely, for this is only a small part of the range of those magnificent words and of the character of God which they reveal.

At root they mean something like 'that which is as it should be'. What does it mean, then, to say that God is righteous? That He sticks to the rules, and plays the game, that He is the perfect gentleman? But the rules are His own.

God does not simply conform to the morality He expects of His people, or exemplify it. He is its source and its *raison d'être*. To say that God is righteous, then, while it certainly implies that He may be relied on not to act unjustly, goes much further. His righteousness is seen not only in His own activity, but in His concern for the activity of His people. They too must keep the rules, and it is the nature of a righteous God to insist that they do. He makes laws to show His people how they ought to live, and He punishes and corrects those who flout His laws. His righteousness is not simply His private character, but is an essential part of His government of His world.

And so it is that the Old Testament presents God as the implacable opponent of injustice and oppression among men. We know it well enough in Amos:

'They sell the righteous for silver,
    and the needy for a pair of shoes –
they that trample the head of the poor into the dust
    of the earth,
    and turn aside the way of the afflicted' (Am. 2: 6, 7).

But it is not only Amos: prophets, poets, and historians unite to declare God's wrath against the man who exploits his neighbour. It comes to a head in the fierce anger with which David heard Nathan's story of the poor man's lamb, and the simple acknowledgment of guilt when Nathan turned it against David himself – 'I have sinned against the Lord' (2 Sa. 12:1-13). The poor man, whom his rich neighbours are able to oppress with impunity, is not too low for the attention of a God whose concern is righteousness. Indeed he is the object of His special care. So much so that the 'meek', the downtrodden poor, emerge in the Psalms as a class who hold a special place in God's affection, and who, by virtue of their situation, may confidently expect

Him to act for them. Their lot may be an unhappy one now, but they will yet have the last laugh:

'Yet a little while, and the wicked will be no more; . . .
But the meek shall possess the land,
  and delight themselves in abundant prosperity'
                                        (Ps. 37:10, 11).

'The Lord lifts up the downtrodden,
  he casts the wicked to the ground' (Ps. 147:6).[10]

Thus the 'righteousness' of God leads inevitably to His deliverance of the oppressed, and this too is included in the meaning of *tsedaqah*; sometimes 'vindication' or even 'salvation' translates it best.

'O Lord, who is like thee,
thou who deliverest the weak
  from him who is too strong for him,
  the weak and needy from him who despoils him?'
                                        (Ps. 35:10).

This is an essential ingredient in *tsedaqah*, for all is not as it should be in the world, and it is the concern of a righteous God to put things to rights.

Particularly is this so where Israel, God's chosen people, is concerned, and it is at this point that *tsedaqah* and *chesed* come close together. Indeed, the former is the consequence of the latter. Because God is faithful in His love for His chosen people, He will not leave them to be oppressed and downtrodden, though they may have fully deserved it, but will vindicate and deliver them. Thus *chesed* in action takes the form of *tsedaqah*, or, as one writer has translated it, 'victorious saving love'.[11]

[10] Many Psalms contain this line of thought; Psalm 10 is a good example.
[11] G. A. F. Knight, *A Christian Theology of the Old Testament* (SCM Press), p. 293.

94

God does not leave a job half done. He does not merely wish that right would prevail; He acts, and when He acts He succeeds. Thus His righteousness issues in triumph, triumph for Himself over all that is not as it should be, and triumph for His people. When God had sent Deborah and Barak to deliver His people from Canaanite oppression, they came back and sang 'the triumphs of the Lord, the triumphs of his peasantry in Israel' (Jdg. 5:11) – and the word is *tsedaqah*, 'righteousness'! In the violent battles of those stormy days, when Israel fought for its very survival, victory was no matter of chance; it was the inevitable outworking of the righteousness of God.

Still more when Israel seemed to have suffered its final eclipse, and the irresistible might of Babylon had reduced the proud people of Yahweh to a gang of slave-labourers, did they cling to the righteousness of God. This was not as it should be; a righteous God could not overlook it. So now, as never before, *tsedaqah* took on the meaning of 'salvation'. Isaiah 51:5-8 is particularly instructive: 'righteousness' in verse 7a translates *tsedeq*, but so also does 'deliverance' in verse 5a. Here it stands parallel with 'salvation', as does *tsedaqah* (also translated 'deliverance') in the refrain at the end of verses 6 and 8. The same word describes both the righteous character of God in which they trusted, and the inevitable practical result of that righteousness in their deliverance. God has not forgotten His people, but will uphold them 'with the right hand of my righteousness' (Is. 41:10, AV), which the RSV correctly translates as 'my victorious right hand'.

This is the range of the 'righteousness' of God as the Old Testament sees it. It is far removed from the crusty image the word conveys to us. His righteousness is not merely a moral rectitude, nor even the stern imposition of such a rectitude on His subjects, but it shades into His love and His faithfulness, as a part of His incredible concern for His chosen people, and issues in His triumphant deliverance of the helpless and the downtrodden. It is a word to strike fear into the wicked and the oppressor, but a word of hope and joy for those who know that right is on their side, for they know that they have not merely the cold approval of a code of law, but the loving concern of a living God.

We have scarcely scratched the surface of the character of God which the Old Testament reveals, but space forbids us to dig any deeper. And however far we explore, there will be more beyond, for God is God and we are men. No mortal man can see the glory of God in its fullness.

Come and stand with Moses on the mountain and learn this lesson. For Moses asked that he might see the glory of God (Ex. 33:18). He did not know what he asked. But God gave him something better still, for as His hand shielded Moses from the burning vision, He gave to his ears a fuller revelation of the true nature of God than ever his eyes could have received. 'The Lord passed before him, and proclaimed, "Yahweh, Yahweh, a God merciful and gracious, slow to anger, and abounding in *chesed* and *emeth*, keeping *chesed* for thousands, forgiving iniquity and transgression and sin, but who will by no means clear the guilty' (Ex. 34:6, 7).

No wonder Moses 'made haste to bow his head toward the earth, and worshipped'. For in that one pregnant sentence stands revealed the heart of the theology of the Old Testament, the mercy and the faithfulness of the sovereign and righteous Lord. And unless we can stand beside Moses, and bow in wonder and reverence before the love of God no less than before His greatness, we have hardly begun to grasp what the Old Testament is about.

6 THREE IN ONE

Our last two chapters, and indeed the majority of the book so far, have been concerned with the revelation of God in the Old Testament. This was no accident. The reason was not so much to register a protest against the tendency of many Christians (in practice, if not in theory) to dismiss the Old Testament and its theology as 'difficult' or 'primitive'; we shall have more to say of this shortly. The reason was simply that it was inevitable. For anyone who wants to discover the biblical teaching about God is driven, whether he likes it or not, to the Old Testament.

The central theme of the Old Testament is God. It records His revelation to Israel of His nature, with the consequent demand for their allegiance, and Israel's progressive discovery, in hard practical experience no less than in thought and worship, of the nature of the God who had made them His own. We have been thinking of some of this discovery in the preceding chapters.

The New Testament does not wipe the slate clean. It does not need to start from scratch. It is the work of men to whom the Old Testament, with all the riches of its teaching about God, was familiar ground. It could be, and it was, taken as read. It is the foundation on which they built, and they found no need to re-lay it.

So you will never work out a biblical doctrine of God from the New Testament alone. In fact you will not arrive at a truly New Testament doctrine of God from the New Testament alone, if by this you mean an understanding of God as the writers of the New Testament understood Him. Unless you start where they started, and make the Old Testament your required reading, you will never share their thoughts. For in the Old Testament is the detailed revelation of the nature of God which they assumed, and on which they based their understanding of the unique events they had witnessed. Their writings are full of hints and allusions, but for the open statement of their doctrine you will need to turn to the source of those allusions, the Old Testament.

There have always been Christians who did not like the Old Testament, and tried to ignore it. One of the most thorough was the heretic Marcion in the second century. He said the God of the Old Testament was not the same person as the loving Father of Jesus, and he dispensed with the Old Testament as a crude and regrettable phase on the path to true religion. But he found he could not stop there, for his New Testament was stuffed with references to the Old Testament. This he blamed on Judaizing Christians who had corrupted the pure teaching of Jesus, who came to liberate men from the vengeful God of the Old Testament, and of Paul, the only apostle who had remained true to his Master's rejection of the Old Testament. So Marcion set to work with his red pencil, and produced a 'purified' New Testament, consisting of duly expurgated versions of the Gospel of Luke and ten letters of Paul. Even then he must have been hard put to it to keep the Old Testament out of sight.

We may laugh at the absurdity of Marcion's attempt. He had as much chance of succeeding as anyone who tries to expurgate references to the Bible from *Pilgrim's Progress*. But there are still too many Marcions about, people who read the New Testament in blinkers, pretending that it can be divorced from the Old Testament, and who talk patronizingly about the Old Testament as one might talk of a child's first attempts at drawing. Of course there is much wonderful new revelation in the New Testament – Jesus did not come for nothing. But the New Testament would be scandalized at the thought that it is new in the sense of rendering the Old Testament obsolete or irrelevant. It is new in the sense of building higher on a solid and reliable foundation.

And as far as the teaching about the nature of God is concerned, the New Testament is clearly well satisfied. It sees little need to amplify, let alone correct, the impression given by the Old Testament. On other matters it has much to add, but on the nature of God it is content to endorse and restate the same truths, and to take them as read. It would take us a long time to trace in detail this endorsement of the Old Testament portrait of God, and it is hardly necessary. Even a superficial reading of the New Testament in the light of such theological ideas as we have been tracing in the Old Testament will reveal the amazing unity of the two parts of the Bible in their understanding of the God who is their chief subject.

God made visible

It may be that the New Testament does not tell us very much about the nature of God which was not already there in the Old Testament, but it does record how that revelation was given in a startlingly new way. For 'In many and various ways God spoke of old to our fathers by the prophets; but in these last days he has spoken to us by a Son' (Heb. 1:1, 2). God no longer simply *told* His people about Himself, or even showed them by His actions. He came Himself, and walked among them, and men *saw* the invisible, God in a human body, the ultimate anthropomorphism. We have pondered this great climax to the revelation of God in an earlier chapter.[1] Here we must simply note that it was in Jesus Christ that all the rich Old Testament revelation of God became focused. Men could look at Him and see, as far as the limitations of a human existence allowed, what God is really like.

But what they saw was not some brand-new god, still hot from the fire in which he was shaped, but the familiar form of the God of Abraham, Isaac, and Jacob, the God of the Exodus and of the Exile, the God of the Old Testament. They saw the same dynamic, irresistible God, as holy, pure, and powerful as ever, and as deeply concerned with and active in the lives of His people. They saw His righteousness blazing out in anger against the Pharisees, and His mercy and vindication extended to the downtrodden and despised. They saw His *ahabah* choosing publicans and sinners to be His followers, and His *chesed* pursuing them through incomprehension, obstinacy, and desertion. And on the lake and on its shores they saw the Creator's power over the winds and waves, and the loaves and fishes, that He had made. We could prolong the list, but the point is clear, that in Jesus Christ we have not a new God, but a new and wonderful way of letting men see the God they had known through Moses and the prophets.

A second God?

'I and the Father are one', said Jesus, and gradually His followers came to see that it was true, and that 'he who has seen me has seen the Father'. It was no easy idea to come to terms with, that they had been eating, sleeping, walking, and laughing with . . . God Himself. But eventually it

[1] See above, pp. 46-48.

dawned on them that they had in fact the unique privilege of seeing God in human form among them.

A privilege, but also a problem. For Jesus talked about God as His Father, and even talked *to* God as His Father. And they knew He was not talking to Himself. But in that case they were dealing not with one God, but with two.

No sooner could such an idea occur to any respectable Jew than he would do his utmost to drive such blasphemy from his mind. 'Hear, O Israel: the Lord our God is one Lord' (Dt. 6:4). 'I am the Lord, and there is no other, besides me there is no God' (Is. 45:5). A score of such uncompromising pronouncements would spring up in his mind to expel the disgraceful idea of a second God. For was it not the very foundation-stone of Israel's faith that their God was alone and unique? Other nations might claim to have other gods, but they had no real existence or power, and a god without power is not a god (see Ps. 96: 4, 5; Is. 44:6-8 and many other passages).[2] To entertain for one moment the idea of a second God was to jettison the whole structure of Old Testament theology, and to forfeit any claim to belong to Israel, the people of the one true and living God.

It was this problem, and it is not a slight one, which led the New Testament writers to make their one great contribution to the biblical doctrine of God, the idea of the Trinity. For this is a biblical doctrine, inescapably present in the New Testament. True, it is for the most part only there in embryo, and the fully developed doctrine of the Trinity was the work of later generations in the church. But we hope to show that the Trinity was not the brainchild of Athanasius or any other philosophical genius. It was there in the data of the New Testament, and the New Testament writers, however little they might have thought through its

[2] See above, pp. 21-22.

implications, were well aware that in the one true God there must be room for the Father, and the Son, and the Holy Spirit. To the Trinity, then, we now turn.

The doctrine of the Trinity

If a popularity poll were taken among the doctrines of the Christian faith, there is little doubt which would come bottom. Nobody likes the doctrine of the Trinity.

To some it is a puzzle, which affronts their intellectual integrity. Three into one won't go, and no amount of philosophical juggling can dispose of the uneasy feeling that the church through nineteen centuries has been talking a lot of highly sophisticated nonsense.

To some it is a scandal. Muslim and Jew join in their scornful rejection of Christianity as a serious contender for the title of top religion. We Christians are still polytheists.

To some it is a joke.

To most it is an embarrassment. They know they ought to believe it because Christians always have, and they do their best, though they are not quite sure what they mean by 'three in one and one in three'. They think up various analogies to make the pill a bit easier to swallow: the sham-rock leaf which is three leaves in one; the divided triangle which is both three triangles and one triangle; the root, the shoot, and the fruit; the fact that H_2O can be liquid (water), solid (ice), or gas (steam). There are plenty more, and we all know them. And most of us find them quite as embar-rassing as the doctrine itself. For one thing, they are not true analogies, and if you press them they will each lead you into some dire heresy. But worse still, they all leave you asking 'Why?'. Why go to all this trouble to find analogies for an idea which seems improbable in its own right? Is it a necessary doctrine? Can't we dispense with it and save all the embarrassment? To these questions the analogies have no answer.

All these attitudes of embarrassment and hostility to the idea of the Trinity are basically due to a failure to realize why the doctrine was ever formulated. It was not that certain Christian thinkers decided to work out a formula which would puzzle and scandalize, nor is the whole thing a practical joke in the worst of taste. The doctrine of the Trinity is the church's way of trying to explain certain very basic facts of Christian experience. It arose because it could not be avoided; the facts had to be accounted for somehow, and there was no other way.

That is why to approach this doctrine by way of philosophical speculation or dubious analogies is at best unhelpful. The only way to get it straight is to go back to the source, and try to relive the tension between belief and experience in the early church which gave rise to it. In other words, the way of approaching this doctrine which gives most hope of reaching a satisfying conclusion is to approach it biblically, for it is in the pages of the New Testament that we see the ferment of revolutionary new ideas which gave rise to this most unexpected of doctrines. And as we do so, we shall find that it belongs not to the cold detachment of the philosopher's study, but to the warm and living experience of the man who has come to know Jesus Christ as the divine Redeemer, and in whose life the Holy Spirit has made God a reality.

Diversity in unity

Before we examine the birth of the doctrine of the Trinity in the New Testament, it is worth noticing that it may not, at least need not, have been quite such a shock to the staunchly monotheistic Jews as we imagine. For the Old Testament gives more than a hint that the 'oneness' of God is not a monolithic and indivisible unity.

We are not thinking here of the places where God apparently speaks of Himself in the plural, or even confers with Himself (Gn. 1:26; 3:22; 11:7; Is. 6:8). These have in the past been triumphantly exhibited as proofs of the Trinity, but they could as well be uses of the 'royal we', or possibly include references to the angels. But there are more substantial indications in the Old Testament of what might be called a plurality, or a diversity, in the Godhead.

There is first of all the fact that God is not alone in His heaven. He is the Lord of hosts, surrounded by a court of angels who do His pleasure, the armies of heaven.[3] Whether or not it was this 'host of heaven' to whom the 'we' passages above were addressed, they are, at the least, frequently in on God's plans, and the agents of their execution. Sometimes they are referred to as 'sons of God',[4] or even as 'gods' (so probably in Pss. 8:6; 82:1, 6).

In fact there is a bewildering variety in the language the Old Testament uses about God and His angels, and it is not always clear which is being referred to. The confusion is increased by the fact that the normal word for 'God' in Hebrew is a plural word, which may not be without its significance for our present enquiry. We cannot go into details here, but must simply notice that this phenomenon has led some scholars to see a 'family relationship within the nature of God',[5] and to paraphrase Lord of hosts as 'Yahweh *who is* hosts'. The case may have been overstated, but it cannot be ignored.

More important is the appearance frequently throughout the Old Testament of one particular 'angel of Yahweh'. He

[3] See, *e.g.*, 1 Ki. 22:19ff.; Is. 6:2, 3; Pss. 89: 5-8; 103:20, 21.
[4] Jb. 1:6; 38:7; Pss. 29:1; 89:6.
[5] G. A. F. Knight, *A Biblical Approach to the Doctrine of the Trinity* (Oliver and Boyd), pp. 21-22. See *ibid.*, pp. 18-25, for a presentation of this point of view.

first appears to Hagar in Genesis 16:7-14, and she concludes that she has seen God (verse 13). Moses saw him in the burning bush, and 'was afraid to look at God' (Ex. 3:2-6), and Manoah, when he recognized the angel of Yahweh, said, 'We shall surely die, for we have seen God' (Jdg. 13:21, 22).

On several of the occasions when he appears, while clearly in the form of a man, he is yet no less than God, and the narrative frequently alternates between referring to him as the angel and as the Lord. Most remarkable is the visit to Abraham before the destruction of Sodom (Gn. 18), where 'three men' appeared to him. In the ensuing narrative plural and singular alternate strangely, and in verse 13 the speaker is Yahweh. Then 'the men', later identified as the 'two angels' (19:1), set out for Sodom, but Abraham continues talking with Yahweh. Early Christian preachers who saw here the three Persons of the Trinity were no doubt putting doctrine before exegesis; but the passage certainly suggests a 'plurality' in God. The angel, it seems, is no less than Yahweh Himself appearing in human form. He is the 'alter ego',[6] the 'double of Yahweh'.[7]

And yet there is a distinction. While Yahweh Himself is said to be in the pillar of cloud and fire (Ex. 13:21; 14:24), at other times it is the angel (Ex. 14:19; Nu. 20:16), and in Exodus 33:2, 3 Yahweh says explicitly that the angel will go before them, but He Himself will *not* go with them. In Exodus 23:20, 21 the angel is sent by God, whose name is in him.[8] So while the angel is certainly a manifestation of Yahweh, and can even be called Yahweh, they are not to be simply identified. This mixture of unity and distinction is fruitful ground not only for the idea of diversity in the

[6] G. A. F. Knight, *ibid.*, p. 30. *Cf.* pp. 25-26 for details of some passages concerned with the angel of Yahweh.

[7] E. Jacob, *Theology of the Old Testament* (ET, Hodder and Stoughton), p. 77.

[8] *Cf.* also Nu. 22:31.

Godhead, but also for the revolutionary idea that God could appear in human form and yet be truly God. While again we must reject, as a matter of exegesis, a simple identification of the angel of Yahweh with the second Person of the Trinity, such a background of thought is hardly irrelevant to our subject.

But the angel does not stand alone as an *alter ego* of Yahweh. We have already considered the characteristically Hebrew idea of the *word* as an almost independent entity, an active extension of the personality of the one who utters it.[9] The word of God is not a mere intellectual concept, but God Himself in action in His world.

Even more strikingly the Spirit of God in the Old Testament is an agent who is sent forth by God and acts decisively for God from Genesis 1:2 on. And yet the Spirit is God Himself in action, not merely an influence or an impersonal servant of God, but God Himself. Of many passages that could be mentioned, consider Isaiah 63:7-14, and note how the same activities are ascribed both to God Himself and to the Spirit. The word and the Spirit are, as it were, extensions of God's personality, God Himself in action, and yet somehow having a distinct existence, and active in their own right. To call them 'persons' would be to fit a Semitic way of thinking into Western logical categories. Let us simply say that, hard as it may be for us to grasp it, the Hebrews did not find it hard to think of the one God as being manifested in various agencies with an almost independent existence.

Space forbids us to pursue this line of thought, as it applies also to the wisdom of God (especially in Pr. 8), the name of God, the glory of God, and the face (or presence) of God. G. A. F. Knight in his book quoted above, *A Biblical Approach to the Doctrine of the Trinity*, sets out the evidence concerning each of these concepts and their relevance to the

⁹ See above, pp. 42-46.

idea of a diversity in the unity of God. It is an exercise which the Western mind finds exhausting, but, at least in the present writer's case, exhilarating. Knight may have gone too far, but he is nearer to a sympathetic understanding of Hebrew thought than those who would constrict the rich diversity of the Old Testament view of God into a monolithic mathematical unit.

This is not to say that the doctrine of the Trinity is a logical development from the Old Testament idea of God. It took the coming of Christ and the experience of the work of the Spirit in the early church to reveal that. But it was probably not so difficult for the Jews to accept a diversity in the one God as we imagine. Indeed, it has been said, with pardonable oversimplification, that the New Testament does not so much expand one God into three Persons, as narrow down a rich diversity within the Old Testament idea of God to a mere Trinity!

Three Gods?

But the fact remains that the first Christians were faced with a problem. They believed in one God, and they found themselves compelled to see Jesus as no less than God as well. We cannot here go into the New Testament evidence for the deity of Jesus. That has been more than adequately covered in other books.[10] Nor can we trace the way they came to see the Holy Spirit as a distinct Person, no less truly divine.[11] Let us content ourselves with observing again that these were not ideas evolved in detached meditation or concocted at a study desk. They were forced on the often unwilling disciples by the sheer facts. They lived with

[10] See especially Leon Morris, *The Lord from Heaven* (Inter-Varsity Press).
[11] See Leon Morris, *Spirit of the Living God* (Inter-Varsity Press).

Jesus, saw all He did, heard all He said, and could come to no other conclusion. They *had* to see in His life the presence of God among them. They could not help worshipping Him, whatever the theological consequences.

When He left them, He promised to send Another to take His place, to continue His teaching and His work. And as they experienced the work of the Holy Spirit in their own transformed lives and in the incredible power of the infant church, once again they recognized God at work among them, and saw that Jesus' promise was fulfilled. The Holy Spirit could have no less honour, no inferior status, come what may. And so, in the exhilarating and unforgettable experience of those early days, when heaven and earth touched, the doctrine of the Trinity was born.

The relationship of the three Persons

But they were not left with the simple and uncomfortable fact of three divine Persons to grapple with. The all-important question was, and is, the relationship of the three Persons to each other, and here they were not left in the dark.

Again there is not space to go into much detail.[12] On the one hand they recognized that Jesus claimed to exercise functions which were properly God's alone, judging, forgiving, giving life, *etc.*, and they knew from their own experience that these claims were true; further, they had heard Him say, 'I and the Father are one', 'He who has seen me has seen the Father', and many similar statements. On the other hand, He spoke often of His dependence on the Father, and obedience to the Father's will, of being

[12] For a detailed account, see A. W. Wainwright, *The Trinity in the New Testament* (SPCK), chapters 10-12. Wainwright's book is an excellent full treatment of this subject.

sent by the Father, and bringing men to the Father; and they heard Him pray for strength, and even plead for a change in the Father's plan, and they knew this was no play-acting. Most terribly of all they heard Him cry, 'My God, my God, why hast thou forsaken me?' but a short time later calmly commend His spirit into His Father's hands. Thus there was unity, but also a very real distinction.

The idea which more than any came to sum up this paradox was that of Father and Son. It was Jesus' own language, and His followers took it up and found it profoundly satisfying. It spoke of His unity with God in the closest family relationship (and remember that for a Jew 'son of . . .' meant 'having the same nature as . . .'), and yet of a degree of interaction, and dependence, which in no way diminishes that unity. It is probably as near as human language can get to doing justice to the facts as Jesus Himself revealed them, and it is His own language.

So far so good, but where does the Holy Spirit fit into this family pattern? Here there is no ready-made extension of the analogy, but again the New Testament gives plenty of indication of the nature of the relationship, particularly between Jesus and the Spirit. (The relation of the Spirit with the Father is less of a problem, and follows quite naturally once this is settled.)

Again, we have no space for full details, but we may note, for instance, that the Spirit is not only the Spirit of God, but the Spirit of Jesus (Acts 16:7; Rom. 8:9; Gal. 4:6; Phil. 1:19); that the life of the Christian is both 'in Christ' (a phrase often used by Paul) and 'in the Spirit' (Gal. 3:3; 5:16, 25, *etc.*); that both the Spirit and Christ make intercession for us (Rom. 8:26, 34). Above all, we may study Jesus' words about the coming of the Spirit in John 14-16, and see how the Spirit comes from the Father at the Son's request, and in His name, and takes over the functions Jesus has been exercising, witnessing to Jesus and taking His teaching and revealing it to the disciples. The unity of the three Persons in this revealing work is well summed up in John 16:15: 'All that the Father has is mine; therefore I said that he (the Spirit) will take what is mine and declare it to you.'

This unity of function between the Spirit and the Son is so close that some have taken it that the Spirit is not really a distinct Person, but just a term for the continuing work of the ascended Jesus, and they have pressed the term 'Spirit of Jesus' into this meaning.[13] But there is clearly a distinction. The Spirit was the agent in the conception of the man Jesus (Mt. 1:18, 20; Lk. 1:35), came on Him at His baptism (Mk. 1:10, *etc.*), and anointed Him for His ministry (Lk. 4:18). Jesus talked on several occasions of the Spirit as a distinct Person (Mt. 12:28; Mk. 3:29; 13:11, *etc.*), and especially with reference to His work after His own departure from the earthly scene – the Spirit was to be sent by Jesus, in His place, to witness to Him, and so on (Jn. 14-16, *passim*).

So we have in the New Testament all the materials for a full-blown doctrine of the Trinity – three Persons, each fully divine in nature and function, closely related to one another, to the point of unity, and yet clearly distinct to the extent of having a real interaction and a relationship of dependence and an order of 'priority'.

But is that as far as it goes? Does the New Testament merely provide the raw materials, or is there at least a trace of the finished product? To this question we finally turn.

---

[13] Use has also been made of the phrase in 2 Cor. 3:17, 'The Lord is the Spirit'; but it is unlikely that 'Lord' here refers to Jesus. The reference is probably to the use of 'Lord' in the preceding allusion to Ex. 34:34; see A. W. Wainwright, *op. cit.*, pp. 215-217.

The Trinity in New Testament thought

To the modern Christian the phrase 'Father, Son, and Holy Spirit' comes easily and naturally. Behind it lie centuries of theological teaching and debate. It is part of our stock-in-trade. And when we meet it in the New Testament we do not turn a hair. 'Go therefore and make disciples of all nations, baptizing them in the name of the Father and of the Son and of the Holy Spirit' (Mt. 28:19). 'But of course,' we think, 'how else?'

Yet really this is staggering, that so soon the three Persons should not only be bracketed together, but even combined in what looks like a regular formula. Just think of the implications. This is the God to whom these new converts were to pledge their allegiance – the Father, the Son, and the Holy Spirit. Behind such an affirmation stands more than a few muddled theological gropings, something much more like a developed doctrine of the Trinity.

Equally formal, and apparently a part of accepted Christian phraseology, is Paul's conclusion to 2 Corinthians: 'The grace of the Lord Jesus Christ and the love of God and the fellowship of the Holy Spirit be with you all.' Already, then, formulae of greeting and worship were beginning to reflect an acceptance of the three Persons as together constituting the Christian deity. Revelation 1:4, 5 shows a similar formula of greeting, though cast in terms of the book's peculiar imagery and phraseology.

Indeed, it seems that it was not uncommon for the thought of the New Testament writers to fall, consciously or not, into a threefold pattern, with reference to the three Persons of the Trinity, not only in formal greetings but in teaching, especially when recounting the wonder of our salvation. They delighted to show how each of the three Persons has a part to play in the great plan.

Thus Peter describes Christians as those 'chosen and

destined by God the Father and sanctified by the Spirit for obedience to Jesus Christ and for sprinkling with his blood' (1 Pet. 1:2), and Paul gives thanks for the Thessalonian Christians, 'because God chose you from the beginning to be saved, through sanctification by the Spirit . . . so that you may obtain the glory of our Lord Jesus Christ' (2 Thes. 2:13, 14). Similar formulae are found in Titus 3:4-6 and Jude 20, 21.

More elaborately, Paul devotes the first chapter of Ephesians to a magnificent exposition of the Christian's salvation, which falls into the same threefold pattern, verses 3-6 telling of the Father's choice, verses 7-12 of the Son's redemption, and verses 13, 14 of the Spirit's sealing, each section concluding with the formula, 'to the praise of his glory'.[14] This pattern enters also into Paul's description of the origin of spiritual gifts (1 Cor. 12:4-6), and of the basis of Christian unity (Eph. 4:4-6), and most thrillingly into his prayer for the Ephesian Christians (Eph. 3:14-19), that they may know the strength of the Spirit within, that Christ may dwell in their hearts, and that they may be filled with all the fullness of God. The true Christian experience is nothing less than being possessed by each of the three Persons of the Godhead. And did someone say that the doctrine of the Trinity was *dull*?

Alongside these passages where a relatively formal threefold pattern of thought is clear, we may mention a large number of places where the three Persons are mentioned together. Many of these may be quite unconscious, the coincidence being dictated by the subject-matter, but certainly this is not always so. Some of the most impressive of such 'coincidences' are the following: Matthew 12:28; Mark 1:10, 11; Luke 1:35; John 1:33, 34; 20:21, 22; Acts

[14] A similar structure has been seen in Rom. 1-8; 1-18-3:20, the judgment of God; 3:21-8:1, justification through faith in Christ; 8:2-30, life in the Spirit.

2:33, 38, 39; Romans 8:11; 15:16, 30; 2 Corinthians 1: 21, 22; Galatians 4:6; Ephesians 2:18; 1 John 4:13, 14. It is hard to believe that some of these do not betray conscious thought about the relation of the three Persons to one another, at least in their activity, if not in their essential nature.

Even the most entrenched resistance to the idea of a doctrine of the Trinity in the New Testament, if it can survive all the evidence above, must surely collapse before the onslaught of the *locus classicus* on the subject, John 14-16. We have already referred to this passage, and cannot hope to do justice to it here, but it cannot be disputed that here is not just an accidental mention of the three Persons together, nor even a set formula, but a consciously thought-out doctrine of their relationship to each other. The following verses in particular bring the three together in a consistent scheme of 'priority' and 'dependence': John 14:16, 26; 15:26; 16:15. We can do no more than urge the reader who is not yet convinced to study these chapters, and to ask himself, 'Has my understanding of the Trinity, after nineteen centuries of Christian discussion and teaching, progressed beyond these deceptively simple words? Have I penetrated closer to the real nature of God than John had?' It will be a humbling exercise.

The New Testament, we may confidently affirm, presents us with a doctrine of the Trinity, and it does so in such a way as to make it clear that this is no optional extra. It is part and parcel of being a Christian. Until you have a doctrine of the Trinity, you have not come to terms with your Christian faith and your Christian experience. And when you do, you will find that the New Testament gives you all you need for a satisfactory understanding. Less than this will not do; and it is a question whether anything more than this is needed.

Conclusion

The Catechism of the Church of England, that little-known and little-used document, has many virtues, not least of which is its summary of Christian belief as enshrined in the Apostles' Creed. It falls into a Trinitarian form:

> 'First, I learn to believe in God the Father, who hath made me, and all the world.
>
> Secondly, in God the Son, who hath redeemed me, and all mankind.
>
> Thirdly, in God the Holy Ghost, who sanctifieth me, and all the elect people of God.'

This summary has the ring of authentic New Testament doctrine. It approaches the Trinity not as a philosophical puzzle, but as a framework into which may be fitted the broad expanse of the dealings of God with His world. Like Paul's uses of the threefold pattern, it is full of the wonder of the comprehensive scope of God's saving work. And above all, it is personal. It speaks of what each Person of the Trinity has done, and is doing, for *me*.

The man who will get the nearest to understanding the Trinity as the New Testament understands it is not the philosopher or the historian, but the man who knows for himself the God who made him, who has redeemed him, and whose power is undeniably producing in his life the fruit of holiness. He is the man who can read the New Testament and say, 'This is where I belong; this is the life I know.' And he is the man to whom the doctrine of the Trinity, while it may stretch his mind to the limit and beyond, is a warm, living, vital echo of his authentic Christian experience. And as he comes to see it in this light, he will realize that the early Christians did not invent this doctrine from sheer cussedness, to make the faith as difficult and unreasonable as they could, but that it forced itself on them, as part and parcel of a revolutionary new way of seeing things, the only way they could account for what God had done, and was still doing, for *them*. And as he sees the doctrine in this light, he will thank God for it, and rejoice in the loving, redeeming, sanctifying work of the triune God.

'God is very kind and good and handsome too. God has given me and some people what we want. He is good. I think He has a white coat and black hair.'

'God is the Father of Jesus. I like God because He puts ideas into my head when I am in trouble with my sums. Jesus is kind because He helps people who are sick.'

'I think that God is a very nice man and is very kind to everyone. Even when you or I do something wrong God will forgive us. He punishes people when they do something very bad. He invented schools.'

'I think God is like us. He is very kind to animals.'

These are some accounts by nine-year-old children of the God they believe in.[1] Adults would not have been so frank, and might have been more sophisticated. But is it not true that man, left to himself, makes God in his own image, in terms of his own tastes and desires and needs? Is not this the sort of God most modern men worship, if they have a God at all?

It is a question whether such a God, a mere projection of human wishes and ideals into infinity, is worth preserving.

[1] Excerpted from an article in the educational magazine *Where?* no. 24, pp. 22-23.

How much practical difference does He make to His devotees? He is no doubt a convenient adjunct to the stiff upper lip as a sanction for the 'British way of life'. In the armed forces church parade on Sundays was once, if it is no longer, a valuable buttress for discipline and morale. But would it make a lot of difference if an atheistic ideology took the place of the kind old man of heaven? The Roman gods seem to have served the army of their day equally well until the politicians found the ideal prescription in the worship of the emperor.

This, I take it, is the starting-point of the idea of the death of God. God, as a living force, *is* dead for the vast majority of the Western world. All that is left is a perfunctory nod to the human ideals to which His name has been transferred. In the practical business of living from day to day, and in modern man's thoughts about the way his world runs, God has no place.

More seriously, much the same could be said of large sections of the Christian church. The *name* of God is still alive, of course; but what does it mean? Is it not too often simply a name added to give a dimension of seriousness and solemnity, perhaps of mystery as well, to what we are saying; or perhaps a convenient way of shelving an awkward question? But what of the *Person* to whom the name belongs? How many of us know Him, and think in terms of His acting in a discernible way above and beyond the normal processes of human life?

Put it this way: can all our God-talk be translated into terms of human experience, psychology, values, *etc.*, *without remainder*? If it can, then could it not be that for us God *is* dead, a superfluous term which would be better removed from our vocabulary, an unnecessary hypothesis?

I think this is what J. A. T. Robinson was getting at in his insistence that we must get rid of the idea of a God 'out there'. The modern world no longer has room for a God who is not fully translatable into human secular language. He must be discarded.

Yet some of us do still want to speak of a God 'out there', or even 'up there'. Of course we do not mean these terms to be taken literally, nor do we imagine that anyone with even an inkling of true religion ever did mean them literally. This, like so much of our vocabulary, is picture language, and none the worse for that. (Try taking any paragraph of a daily paper and eliminating all the metaphors, and you will soon be convinced that, tidy as it might be to speak only in dead literal terms, it would make conversation very tedious – and probably impossible!) What we mean by it is that God is transcendent (an equally spatial metaphor!), that He is not man, that He exists independently of the universe He has made, and is not to be identified with it, or with any part of it, or even with any principle of its working. He is a distinct, real, living Person, who may be known personally, and who acts in a practical, discernible way in the universe.

This, very inadequately, is the sort of idea that 'out there' language was coined to convey. It was never intended to be taken in literal spatial terms, any more than phrases like 'high ideals', 'low morals', 'upgrading', 'the sky's the limit', or even the idea of depth. (It is amusing to see that many theologians who scornfully repudiate 'out there' language cheerfully substitute the no less spatial metaphor of depth!) It describes that which falls outside the scientifically observable, empirical world of man's experience. Or, to use an equally maligned expression, it describes the supernatural.

To reject the idea of God 'out there' is to eliminate the supernatural, to reduce the whole field of religious thought and language to purely empirical terms, to a rather complicated way of talking about man and his concerns and his world, and nothing more.

Now this is nothing new. It was what the old-fashioned

liberals wanted to do, and they did it by the simple expedient of denying the miraculous element in Christianity, rejecting supernatural language, and working with a drastically expurgated Bible.

It is what the modern existentialist theologians are after, but they opt for the more hazardous method of 'demythologizing', of trying to reinterpret supernatural language, which is not a thought-form that means anything to modern man, and to see what content they can give to that language which will be acceptable to the secular mind. Hardly surprisingly, the result is a Christianity which bears a remarkable resemblance to secular existentialism.

This too is what the death-of-God men want, and they effect the removal of the supernatural more radically (and, it may be suggested, more honestly) by the simple elimination of God-language, though they still cling to much of the traditional language and thought of Christianity.

This, finally, is the avowed aim of the humanists, and they at least are completely open and above board. Religious language as a whole, and of course God with it, must go. The supernatural was an illusion from the start. There is no more to reality than what man sees, feels, thinks, and aspires to. The ultimate reality is man.

To all these schools of thought, the idea of a transcendent, personal, living God, of a God who is real and active, and who does not fit comfortably into the categories of the secular mind, is anathema. He is an anachronism in this modern world. Man, now that he has come of age, has no place for such a God. Let Him be crucified.

This should be no surprise to us. The fact that men today do not find the biblical idea of God credible is nothing new – the majority of men never have. What *is* surprising and dismaying is that this rejection of a supernatural God is now more plausible, since so many of those who purport to be His servants show no more sign of believing in such a

God in practice than do their secular neighbours. Until the Christian church rediscovers the living God, we can hardly expect the rest of the world to take Him seriously.

But let it be firmly stated and squarely face up to that the Bible from Genesis to Revelation is stiff with supernatural ideas and language. To try to 'demythologize' it is to try to impose on it an alien thought-form, the secular viewpoint of the modern Western world. It is like trying to reinterpret the world of Winnie-the-Pooh in terms of thermodynamics. To attempt such a transplant on to the Bible is to invite immediate rejection; the tissues do not match. The language of the Bible is quite inappropriate to express what modern secular man wants to say about his world, and to try to make it do so is to invite confusion, double-think, and hypocrisy.

It is far better to take the honest path of humanism, to make a clean breast of it, and leave God out altogether. Talk, if you will, of existential experience and depth psychology, but do not use the word 'God' to describe what *man* thinks and feels. The word 'God', and all the super-natural language of the Bible which goes with it, is only appropriate to describe the 'Transcendental Interferer', and that is precisely what none of these schools of thought wants to mention.

It seems, then, that we are left with a stark antithesis. The Bible presents an understanding of reality which is anathema to the secular mind, and the secular mind can find no place for the God of the Bible. There are two thought-worlds here, and they are radically at variance.

Can we ever make the Bible mean anything to modern man? Or would we do better to throw in the sponge right away, and, in company with many modern theologians who have confronted humanist thought, since we can't beat 'em, join 'em?

The God of the gaps

Let us be fearlessly honest. It is no good pretending that we are really saying nothing very different from what secular man already believes. When we speak of God we *are* introducing a whole realm of thought which is quite alien to the secular way of seeing things. We *are* talking about a supernatural, transcendent, personal, interfering God, and there is nothing to be gained by trying to camouflage the fact.

How then are we to bridge the gulf between what we as Christians want to say and what the secular mind is prepared to take into consideration?

Some still try to find the answer in the God of the gaps. They go along with secular thinking as far as the point where it runs into obscurity, and then triumphantly proclaim that there must be God. Of course we all repudiate this apologetic in its crude form, but there are many who would point to the world of nature, exposing its immensity and the intricacy of its design to the point where the mind boggles, and then declare, 'Only an almighty God could have made such a universe.'

The cosmological and teleological arguments for the existence of God, which still have their exponents, are really only slightly refined versions of the God-of-the-gaps apologetic. We have seen in chapter 2 that the biblical support for this line of argument, if addressed to the unbeliever, is at least shaky. The universe has much to tell the believer of the greatness of its Creator; but it does not give the unbeliever sufficient cause to postulate a God he has no other reason to believe in. Any scientist will agree that the universe is wonderful, and that he does not understand all about it – not yet at least. But the fact that he has not yet explored all the corners is not sufficient reason to abandon his secular frame of reference and bring in the alien category of the supernatural. The God of the gaps has little biblical support – and in practice He does not cut much ice!

God for modern man

How then can we present the living God to a world which has no room for Him in its thinking? Where, if at all, does He impinge on the world with which secular man is familiar? Will anything convince secular man that he needs to broaden his mind and make room for the supernatural? We make three suggestions, which may be pointers to a more biblical, and a more effective, apologetic in our twentieth-century Western world.

1. God incarnate
Modern man respects what he can see, and hear, and touch. This is reality. He talks, if he is sufficiently sophisticated, about 'empirical verifiability', but if he is a normal human being he simply says with Thomas, 'Unless I see, I will not believe', which comes to the same thing.

But Thomas *did* see, and so did thousands of others. In Jesus God invaded in the most ruthless way the world of sight and sound. God became empirically verifiable. At a fixed point in the world's history there walked a man on earth who said He was God.

Men may ignore theories, and dispute opinions, but if they make any claim to being fair-minded thinkers they cannot shrug off facts. And Jesus is a fact, rooted in the empirical framework of secular history. Facts must be explained, especially such an extraordinary fact as Jesus. Until a man has fairly and objectively examined the fact of Jesus, of what He did, what He said and the impression

He made, and has made a fair and reasonable judgment on what this fact implies, he has no right to write off the whole supernatural world as nonsense. For Jesus' whole life was steeped in the supernatural, and His teaching would make nonsense if you tried to translate it into purely secular terms. The claims He made about Himself are supernatural through and through. You cannot accept Jesus without making room for God, and not just a mealy-mouthed apology for God, but the living God of the Old Testament, no less, a God to be reckoned with, the God who raised Him from the dead.

Here then is the transcendent God in the secular world, empirically verifiable.

2. God in action

Elisha stood by the Jordan with his new mantle in his hand and cried, 'Where is Yahweh, the God of Elijah?' For answer he did not look for a theological treatise, or even a devotional experience – he struck the water, and the water was parted (2 Ki. 2:14).

Here again was empirical evidence, and this sort of evidence too cannot be ignored by secular man. Here again the transcendent invades the material world. Of course men will always try to find another explanation of the work of God, but there comes a point at which it requires more credulity to speak of coincidence than it does to believe in God. At that point, secular man comes face to face with the living God – on his own terms.

What we Christians must do, therefore, is not so much to argue more as to act more, or rather to look for the action of God. We must not be afraid to ask God for specific things, as Elisha did, and to expect an answer which will be visible not only to the eye of faith but also to the sceptical observer. It is valuable, of course, to refer to the experiences of other Christians, the George Müllers and Hudson Taylors. This is good, solid, empirical evidence of a God who is real, a God who can be relied on for practical help. And there are innumerable examples more modern than these: our Christian bookstalls abound with them. But more impressive still is the realization that God does not only answer the prayers of these 'super-saints', but of the ordinary rank-and-file Christian who dares to take Him at His word. We owe it to our sceptical friends not to deny them this evidence.

When men can see Christians who not only talk of knowing God, but clearly believe in a God who *acts*, and when they see that action resulting, then they will find it harder to confine reality within the narrow limits of the secular framework.

3. God in us

When Christians talk about their experience of God, many non-Christians cannot get rid of the sneaking feeling that they are really describing, in unnecessarily obscure and misleading language, the same sort of feelings and experiences that they also know, without any reference to 'God'. Sadly this is sometimes true: the Christian thinks secular man's thoughts after him, and regurgitates them in Christian terminology.

What the non-Christian needs to be able to see, if he is ever to take much notice of our God-talk, is that when we Christians mention God we are talking about someone whom we *know*, and he does not; that our Christian experience is something radically different from his, different in kind, not just in degree.

And in general no amount of sheer talk will make him see this. He will see it, if at all, by what we *are*. When a man can see, in a fellow-human being like himself, a change which is inexplicable within a secular framework, then he may sit up and take notice. Of how many Christians can it be said that they just do not make sense in humanist terms? They are the ones whose talk about God will be listened to.

These are only pointers, very inadequately expressed, to an apologetic for today. The point we wish to make is that the living God of the Bible is a God who acts in a quite undeniable way, a God who interferes, a God who cannot be stowed away in a padded cell labelled 'Metaphysics'. This is the God to whom the Christian church is called to bear witness, and that witness is unlikely to be effective if it is uncertain or apologetic about the reality of God's impact on His world. When secular man can see with his own eyes that God is active right here in the secular world, when he can see fellow-men to whom the supernatural is clearly a vital reality and whose lives bear witness to the God they confess, and when he is prepared to take up the Gospels again and look squarely at the fact of Jesus, then he may begin to realize that

'There are more things in heaven and earth, Horatio,
Than are dreamt of in your philosophy';

that the secular framework of his thinking is not adequate to contain reality as he is coming to be aware of it; that, in fact, God is.

The church today seems to be wallowing in an orgy of self-pity and defeatism. It has given up hope of getting a hearing for its message, and is looking desperately for ways of adapting its message to meet its customers' requirements. And in the process it is in danger of jettisoning not only its theology, but its God.

It is the contention of this book that there is another way, and that way is to return to the living God. He has not changed, and when His people learn again to see Him, as the Bible sees Him, as the unique, transcendent, sovereign Lord, 'who dwells in unapproachable light, whom no man has ever seen or can see', and yet who is dynamically active in His world, the God for whom nothing is too hard, and whose will none can withstand, then the world will not so easily be able to ignore Him.

In other words, the answer is not a new theology, but a new experience of the living God. The church must learn to abandon the secular thought which it hides under a cloak of religious language, and come out unashamedly and openly on the side of a God who acts, a God to be reckoned with. Then it may be that the world will respects its message.

> 'For my people have committed two evils:
>> they have forsaken me,
> the fountain of living waters,
>> and hewed out cisterns for themselves,
> broken cisterns,
>> that can hold no water' (Je. 2:13).

INDEX OF PRINCIPAL BIBLICAL REFERENCES

Incidental references are not included, but only passages cited or discussed verbatim.